TRIUMPH HOUSE
Poetry with a Purpose

REALMS OF FAITH

Edited by

Steve Twelvetree

First published in Great Britain in 2000 by
TRIUMPH HOUSE
Remus House,
Coltsfoot Drive,
Woodston,
Peterborough, PE2 9JX
Telephone (01733) 898102

HB ISBN 1 86161 760 7
SB ISBN 1 86161 765 8

FOREWORD

In today's modern world everyone's life is fast-moving and hectic, leaving little time to stop, open our minds and gather together our thoughts. However, there are times when we really do need to take time out to sort our feelings and emotions. Poetry can very often provide us much-needed release by allowing us to express and share our important thoughts with others.

Realms Of Faith is a special collection of these poems, featuring the work of over 120 new and established authors of today.

Together they combine their creative talents to present to you an inspiring and enjoyable read that you will want to return to time and time again.

Steve Twelvetree
Editor

CONTENTS

A Candle For Prayer

Take up a little candle
And place it where you will
Beside the cross of Jesus
And leave it there until
You've spent some precious moments
In thoughtfulness and prayer
Then like your lighted candle
Leave your burden there

Take up another candle
And leave it in a room
Tinged with fear and loneliness
And with approaching gloom
When the evening shadows gather
And you find it hard to pray
Just close the door behind you
And let the fragrance stay

Take your remaining candles
And when the day is done
Pray for yourself and others
And light them one by one
Then slowly watch the darkness
Give way to fragrant light
And know your prayer will be answered
In the stillness of the night.

C MacIntyre

THE CHURCH

Have you seen the little church
Up there upon the hill
A little place of worship
Just standing very still.

A pretty little steeple
And a bell that often rings
A crowd of willing worshippers
Where people pray and sing.

The mullioned coloured windows
Where the sun comes shining through
It shines just like a rainbow
Making patterns on the pews.

Yes, a little place of worship
The building very old
Where people come to worship
And God's message to unfold.

J Mary Kirkland

NEW LIFE

I have arrived on Earth
My time to be born.
Did you heed Gabriel's horn?
It's time for all to say
Lion lie down with the lamb today.

A Park

DRINK

Drink of the cup O thirsty soul
Refresh the part that yearns.
Sup deep from the eternal spring,
God's strength to thee return.

All ye who take aught yet give nought,
Drink of the stream your all.
Let purity course thro' thy blood
And watch thy burdens fall.

Drink knowledge O thou thirsty soul,
Fear not to close the gate.
For in Christ wisdom thirsteth not
But rests content and sate.

J G Ryder

UNDESERVEDLY

I see my soul's face turn ashen
as I feel I'm treated undeservedly:
no food nor drink will revive her colour
till slowly and painfully I come to realize
that this must be how God is made to feel,
each time we rebel against His love.
Yet He forgives us. Why can't I?
That's why he had to send his only son
to die so undeservedly.

Michiko Araki

MY CONVERSION

For many years I went to church
And took an active part
In all the service of the Lord,
But did not yield my heart.

I worked so hard, but had no time
To stop and think and pray,
I was so busy serving
That I didn't hear God say:

'I died for you, that you might live
And have eternal life,
To know the joy of sins forgiven,
Of victory over strife.'

I was baptised and joined my church,
But God was far from me,
But oh how much He loved me
And longed to set me free.

Then one night at the crossroads,
My soul found sweet release,
I heard the Saviour's loving voice
Say, 'Sinner go in peace.'

My heart is full, for He is mine,
I've joy that knows no end,
For now He lives within my heart,
My Saviour, guide and friend.

D Kirkby

ON THE THRESHOLD OF THE NEW MILLENNIUM

Two thousand years, a mere two seconds in time since
       the world began,
Yet to us it seems, in our world of dreams, the most
       vital two seconds in life.

Our human brain cannot easily grasp there was a time
       when life did not exist:
When we were not alive and may not survive for ever
       or e'en for the next 1000 years!

This particular century, we've made more progress than ever before,
Explored outer space, expanded the human race, yet not learnt
       to be human at all!

We still envy each other's good fortune, jealous when we
       cannot have someone we love,
We still start wars without a cause, and are quick to point a finger
       at anyone we think guilty!

We pollute our lungs with smoke; our cities and our planet
       are choking with rubbish
Thrown carelessly away, despite the fact that we say:
       'Keep Britain Tidy!'

Yet if you look beyond the crass, the selfish, the mercenary,
       the uncaring few,
You'll find life's gift, which will uplift and rest like a jewel
       in the crown!

It may be a child's smile, a trusting paw of your dog or your cat,
Helping hands, or someone who understands and is willing
       to give you some time.

For the new millennium, let's hope cures will be found for
       the world's deadliest diseases;
All wars will cease, we'll live in peace! God's love and tranquillity
       will reign everywhere for all time!

Verica Peacock

GOODBYE, MY SON

You entered the world early
A smiley baby, never surly,
People said you'd wow the girls
With your big brown eyes and darkish curls.
That much was true, a tall, handsome lad
Emerged from the rebellious boy I had.
Our world turned dark when you became ill
In your early twenties, with a life to fulfil.

The years passed, you had no life
Tied to a dialysis machine, you lost your wife.
A transplant gave you a few years' respite
For five short years you enjoyed life at its height
The steroids played havoc from the start,
Skin eruptions, stomach ulcers, then the heart
And to crown it all, the big 'C',
I was devastated, you'd suffered so much misery.

You never did complain,
Always said there was no pain,
But your eyes gave you away, my son,
You didn't want to spoil our fun.
Unselfish to the end, no wonder people loved you.
The hardest thing I've ever had to do
Was the day I had to say 'Goodbye' to you.
My only consolation, your years of pain were through.

R E Downs

DUNBLANE, 13.03.96

(written on the day of the Dunblane massacre)

This morning we lost sixteen children,
More bonny they couldn't have been,
And their teacher - struck down in a frenzy,
The like of which seldom is seen.

The numbness of so many parents
And friends, who are sharing their pain,
Is hard to imagine this evening,
As a quietness rests on Dunblane.

In the future the anguish will deepen,
As the town is transformed overnight,
For tomorrow the key politicians
In this grief-stricken town will unite.

The courage of all who assisted
Those children so young and afraid
Is truly a notable feature
Of the love on this morning displayed.

But what should we feel for the gunman?
His actions we cannot condone,
His mind was clearly in turmoil
And the motive may never be known.

But this we should feel with conviction -
Each traumatised husband and wife
Was granted a rare glimpse of Heaven
In those few precious years of young life.

Margaret Wood

FAITH

The smile was gone from upon her face
She seemed lost or in some distant place.
I called her name, but she turned away,
I begged, 'Don't go, please won't you stay?'
She tried to speak, to tell me why,
She didn't really want to die.
But what is death, it's just a word,
To be scared of it is just absurd.
She turned once more to say goodbye,
This time not a tear she'd cry.
The smile was back upon her face
Because she was going to a better place.
A place where pain it had no right,
A place where fear gave up the fight.
A place called home through heaven's door,
Keep faith as your key
And we'll meet once more.

Maria Urwin

OUR UNSEEN FRIEND

Unhappiness wears many cloaks
Beneath to hide,
The wounded spirit of some grief,
Or love denied,
But all to Him is seen
All known,
Each grief He shares
And with His love,
Will wipe away, those
Hidden tears.

Barbara Grove

A New Beginning

As we start a new millennium
Let's rethink the way we live
Help to heal our sick old world
More love and friendship to give
Show others that we really care
Offer help to someone in need
Let's make a safer place for all
No matter what colour or creed
To preserve the beauty God created
Not to wantonly tear it apart
Give hope to folk who are feeling down
help the homeless have a new start
Lord help us to protect our beautiful world
In this precious life we live
Then as we greet the new millennium
We'll find the strength to give.

Cindy Brewster

A Temple Worthy Of Our Lord

Where is there a temple, worthy of our Lord,
There is St Paul's Cathedral, magnificent, inspired,
Built with human hands long years ago.
God held it in his everlasting arms,
Through times of war, his temple stood.
We in awe, wondered how it was delivered,
Only through God. Our God,
The God of miracles.

Madeline Chase

UNTITLED

I wish to speak of deep things . . .
out of my emptiness
out of my blankness no word comes
           day sounds tumble
           incoherent in my shell
I am part of air in my silence
primitive as first man
as he gazed at the stars
           startling as new fire in his eyes
           a struck match solidifies my senses
           and I become aware of pulse and breath
remembering my name which parts me from you
from trees
      from air
           only to reach out in words
I wish to speak -
I lift up my hands.

B Maskens

IN AWE

There's something up there in the sky,
It could be castles
It might be pie,
The stuff from which our dreams are made,
That keeps us staunch and unafraid
To face the facts and fight the foe,
We should never let it go
That something in the sky.

David Madeira-Cole

A WINTER'S DAY

Snowflakes are falling
Lacy patterns they make
Jack Frost roams about
And there's ice on the lake.

Soon all is covered
In a white, powdery foam
Still smiling bravely
Is Fred, the garden gnome.

The children come laughing
Leaving paper and pen
Throwing snowballs so merrily
And making snowmen.

Pegs on the clothes line
Like brides in their gowns
Are dancing and swaying
Could they be circus clowns?

All thanks for such beauty
And praise to our Father above
For He created the seasons
With an abundance of love.

Eva A Perrin

A Precious Diamond

With precision he cut the diamond,
Sweat stood out on his brow,
For hours and hours he considered
Just where that precious line should be.
In his hand he held a jewel of rare beauty,
As anyone could see.
Months ago, dug up from the depths of the earth,
Men toiled for hours and hours -
Hoping, constantly,
For a jewel so rich, so rare,
In this vision, the future lay before his eyes,
Riches galore, fantastic!
If only he could sell this diamond,
So big, so beautiful, so sparkling,
For all the world to see,
To adorn a rich lady's finger,
Or grace her chest, if in a gold frame it hung, it be.
Maybe placed in a tiara, gleaming
Upon her golden hair,
Then suddenly, with a jerk, he woke up,
Seat pouring from his brow.
Realisation! It was all a dream,
For no jewel in his hand he held.
Goodness! Life could be so cruel, so mean!

Vi Blakeston

A COLD AND COUGH

First my throat is hot and dry,
Then my eyes begin to cry.
Nose is hot and prickly too;
I think I've got a cold, don't you?

I have a heavy, throbbing head,
I feel like taking to my bed;
In fact I'm one enormous ache,
Perhaps an aspirin I will take.

My nose starts running like a tap,
This cold my strength just seems to sap.
My back, it seems, will split in two
- I wonder if I have the 'flu?

Next I get a nasty cough,
And so my scarf I dare not doff:
It helps keep warm my wheezy chest.
I struggle on and do my best.

I cannot breath, my voice is hoarse,
I cough, and cough, and cough, of course.
A few days more and - who can tell -
Perhaps again I may feel well?

Joan Cole

SEVEN RIDDLES OF LOVE

Love is as innocent as a small child
Yet it is wiser by far than the mind.

To love is to trust - take a leap in the dark
Yet be certain inside that it will reach its mark.

The more love is given, abundant it grows
As the flowers spring up the more seed that one sows.

Love not only gives but can freely accept
A gift in return never counted a debt.

Although love is fearless, it fears to offend
Its object a gift not to own but to tend.

True love cannot die yet will lay down its life
It will sacrifice self to disarm any strife.

Love is enduring and endlessly strong
While love can be hurt, it outlasts every wrong.

Jane Bouttell

THE WORD WAS MADE FLESH AND DWELT AMONG US

Was God incarnate only once,
The Christmas Christ of Bethlehem;
That cave and crib a special place
Forever then?

Our being is but one short life,
Sum of its years three score and ten.
Christ seeks rebirth, for each man's heart
Is Bethlehem.

Peter Marshall

HOW MANY?

How many Sundays
In 2000 years.
How many heartaches
How many tears
How many times
Has a Christian prayed
How many times
Has somebody strayed
How many years
Till the fighting is done
How many years
Since the first war begun
How many years
Till all Christians join hands
How many years
Till there's peace in our land

J M Slowley

LIFE

Plump dimpled flesh,
Birth.
New clear eyes, limbs,
Alive.
Waving movements, pushing,
Growing.
Thriving, feeding, learning,
Showing.
The continuity, the explanation;
Life.

Morag Wright

THE BUTTERFLY

As we sang hymns to praise the Lord,
a butterfly came in and soared
above our heads and 'round the room.
This spirit flies on gossamer wings,
wafting high as our hearts sing;
lifted up by the joy of our tune.

Its wings would make a gentle breeze,
as we prayed upon our knees.
Then it would rest upon the wall.
This thing of beauty flew above,
to remind us of the love
of the Lord, who saved us all.

A caterpillar, fat and long,
spun a cocoon of silk so strong.
It slept until the time was right,
then emerged, then took flight.
This resurrection, and rebirth,
reminds us of our Lord while on earth.

Thank You for the sermon You taught.
to bring us peace when with problems we're fraught.
A butterfly; a new creation;
encourages our hopeful anticipation
and overcomes all the delay and fuss.
We know Your Spirit is here with us.

Rosemary Taylor

UNTITLED

Long time ago in Bethlehem
The Christ child babe was born;
In a stable rude and bare
To all the world forlorn;
To seek and save a fallen world
From the grip of sin;
For dying on a cross in shame
Our world He entered in.

It was for you 'Dear friend' He came,
For you He bled and died;
That heaven at last we all might gain
For God is satisfied;
He paid the price to set us free
So we might enter in;
The portals of His heavenly home
Free from the taint of sin.

This Christmas we remember Him,
His lowly birth and share
The happy celebrations thus
Of God's redeeming care;
O trust this Saviour while you may
Who for your sake was born,
Kneel at His cross and take Him thus
New life in you will form.

John Gardiner

In A Letter To My Sweetheart
1932

Spirit and thought are not enough
To keep a half-lit fire from dying -
The tender touch of hand on hand
And deeper, sweeter things . . . are not enough.
You say we must be patient . . .
My plea is that our life is but a scan,
And you . . . are you . . .
And I, for aye, your man.
This wondrous youth
We share, passes like a dream,
So fleeting. In truth
It is the quality of time that counts.
Hours and minutes are a man's device . . .
Life is God's . . .

Leslie Toye

Keeping An Eye

Who looked after the world while I was asleep,
It was still there for someone else to safe keep.

Are we so vital justifying our part,
Someone will carry on when we run out of heart.

Are we missed for what we do, or what we are,
maybe someone somewhere thinks that you are a star.

Many stay in the wings as we perform our act,
Ready to improve on the qualities we lacked.

T A Napper

ONE DAY AT A TIME

Teach me Lord, one day at a time,
To follow your way not just mine
Always be patient wear a smile
Nothing is perfect all the while.

Life's uncertain yes constantly
A bed of roses not meant to be
But blessings truly override
The many problems at one's side.

One day at a time - can't be wrong
Following always the right road on,
Laughing as troubles come your way
Easy no - just life day by day.

P M Peet

WHERE IS HEAVEN?

Earth is a part of heaven,
Like a baby in the womb,
We have to die to live there,
like a baby being born.
He doesn't know what life is like,
Or even want to know
Because he's happy where he is but -
We really need to know
What heaven is like and where,
And how to get there!

B Phipps

CELEBRATING CHRIST'S BIRTHDAY

Two thousand years have come and gone
Since Christ came to this earth
He came to show God's love to all
He came to give new birth.

This is His birthday we celebrate
A birthday filled with joy
To those who know that God is love
May our powers for Him be employed.

Have you accepted this gracious love?
For the years that are to come.
Have you accepted His comforting word
'I will never leave you alone'?

The Bible clearly says that all
At His feet will bow the knee
So put your feet on His gracious path
That will lead you to victory.

The victory was made when we gave our hearts
To our Saviour Jesus Christ.
He won the battle, He rose to save
Those who believe in His sacrifice.

So as the millennium comes in view
May we meet the challenge He gives
He's Lord, He's Saviour, our God made man
Above all He reigns and lives!

K Lethem

THE ARDLEIGH MILLENNIUM GREEN

Every village needs a green,
In Ardleigh one will soon be seen.

Local people plans have scanned,
And long discussions ideas planned.

A plot of land has now been bought,
But further funds must soon be sought.

By giving work, or cash, or seeds,
Our green will soon have what it needs.

So many things we hope to plant,
(Some were donated by my Aunt).

Trees and hedgerows - wild flowers too -
Shrubs and leaves of glowing hue,

Footpaths, maypole, sundial, pond,
Meadow flowers and woods beyond.

There will be space for children's play,
And seats where older folks can stay.

A cycle route, and apple walk,
And shelter, where it needs be sought.

So much to do - how time does fly,
We hope that things won't go awry.

But, when the year 2,000 dawns,
Our lovely green will then be born!

J Wyhowska

EVE TO EVE

A cool evening breeze flutters a flag
On a far away hill the call of a stag
The body now tired, ready for bed
The silhouette clouds set in pink, gold and red.

A quiet time at the death of a day
A moment of thought sometimes you pray
The breeze now more chill, as the night gains its spurs
And its race is now on, till gold morning occurs.

Gold morning you shake off the shackles of night
You warm up the Earth to help nature's fight
A new start, a new hope, you show us the way
As the brightening sky breaks into day.

The day is the time when battles are done
In factories and boardrooms, in shops and in homes
The morning speeds by with energies burst
The afternoons pass with the speed of a hearse.

Then life goes on at a lazier pace
A slowing down time, for some grace
A stroll in the park or across fields of corn
It's goodbye to the day the evening is born.

A cool evening breeze flutters a flag
On a far away hill the call of a stag
The body now tired, ready for bed
The silhouette clouds set in pink, gold and red.

V P Bruce-Jones

THE BIBLE

Do you possess a bible? I sincerely hope you do.
There are many lovely stories written there for me and you.
Stories written long ago proclaiming Christ the king
And how God made the universe and every living thing.
From Genesis to Malachi God's purposes are made,
Telling of a loving Saviour coming as a babe.
In chapter three of Genesis tells how Adam fell,
Eve took the fruit and ate it and tempted him as well.
They both were disobedient bringing sin and shame
Into the world so beautiful, but Satan was to blame,
His craftiness and cunning ways will fill your heart and mind
With evil thoughts and sinfulness and doubts of every kind.
But don't despair, he'll not win through when we have Christ
the king,
He came to earth from heaven above to save us from our sins
The prophesy Isaiah told in verse six, chapter nine,
Has come to pass, a son is given, born of David's line
From Matthew unto Revelations many miracles were performed.
Jesus walked upon the water and calmed the raging storm,
He healed the sick and suffering, He made the blind to see,
Then at the end was crucified and nailed upon a tree.
Yes, the holy book is special, turn the pages everyday
And you will know such joy and peace to help you on your way.

K Godwin

ELEGANCE

She was trés-chic, elegant,
her deportment proud, not arrogant.
Her perfume subtle, pervasive,
her glance direct, but elusive.

She walked to her director's chair,
the light from the window on her hair.
White blouse, black pin-stripe attired,
enhanced the slender figure to be admired.

She looked at each man around,
instant silence, not a sound.
All previous thoughts banished,
any trace of chauvinism vanished.

Their fashion firm was going to seed,
her modern assertiveness was their need.
They were ready to accept the change,
she advocated success and elegance.

Licia Johnston

MAY WE

The glow of dawn
the break of day
God created in His own way.
The silver moon
The stars at night
Seem to reflect Heaven's light.
In this lovely world you gave us
May we add each day,
A measure of love and kindness,
As we travel on life's way.

Nan Ogg

HYMN FOR THE MILLENNIUM

Gracious Lord, eternal Saviour,
Bless all people on the earth
Who in humble adoration
Now commemorate your birth;
Give us wisdom, give us courage,
That in virtue and accord
We may be to all good neighbours,
In the image of our Lord.

Steadfast saints and Christian martyrs
Kept the faith and spread the word,
Thus in every generation
Was the precious gospel heard,
Bringing hope where darkness flourished,
Reaching out to every place,
So in this and all the nations
All might love, and peace, embrace.

Sadly, through the passing centuries
Mankind turned to strife and hate,
Pray forgive the latent evil
We have helped to aggravate;
Boost resolve and banish conflict
Give us grace to start anew,
Ever seeking for your guidance
And the strength to see things through.

Lord of all in true obedience
May we in our day and age,
Help progress your earthly kingdom
Conscious of our heritage;
Gladly raise the torch of freedom
Foster justice, wrongs defy,
Marching forth in Christ's millennium
With your banner hoisted high.

John Pert

DOWN IN MUDDY WATERS

I'm down in muddy waters, the floods sweep me away,
Life is a disaster full of driftwood and decay,
Only you can free me, set me on dry land,
Love and beauty live in you, healing in your hands.

For your love shines like sparkling wine,
Like the jasmine skies at the dawn of time,
Like the misty roses in the gardens at night,
Like the dancing leaves in the autumn light.

You came into my heart like a river clear and blue,
All my lonely life I'd been looking for you,
And though these troubled waters may rage all around,
No one can deny me this new love I have found.

Nigel Evans

A LETTER TO GOD

Dear God - When you created me inside my mother's womb
You knew what fate awaited me from cradle to the tomb;
You knew the pressures life would bring with which I'd have to cope
That's why you gave me faith, dear God, and why you gave me hope.

You knew that many'd fall away although at birth we're pure,
You knew that most of us would quickly fall for life's allure,
You knew that I would need your help, alone I couldn't cope:
I thank you that you gave me faith and that you gave me hope.

Geoff Tullett

THE EAGLE

Soaring, wheeling in the air,
Jubilant and free,
Lifted by the Spirit's power
Christ calls me to be.
Like an eagle, strong and whole
I am made to soar
Far above the things of earth,
All I've known before.

Not on my own faltering wings,
But with strength divine
He will bear me up aloft
By His great design.
Borne on thermals of His grace,
I view from above
All the trials that I face
Touched with Christ's own love.

Ann Clifton

THE RAINBUSH

Festooned chains of silver tears
  Crystal backdrop to a darkening sky
    Each clear pearl from heaven sent
      Striking sweet chords from leaf to leaf
        Perfect pitch of orchestration
          Wild metronome of nature
            Conducting musically each jewel
              Waiting suspended for a turn
                To fall and quench the earth below

Jane Manning

IS IT REAL?

'I wonder if it's real?' she said
As she gazed into the store,
'I'd buy it if I thought it was,
I could really do with some more.'

She was talking of teddy bears you see,
The ceramic kind of thing
That children and adults collect,
Much happiness they bring.

But some are false, just plaster made,
Would crumble if they fell,
Just like so many worldly things
That send someone to hell.

If only we would realize
That Jesus is for real,
he died for us, He loves us so,
Forgives our sins, our hurts He'll heal.

All we've to do is ask Him in,
Into our hearts today,
Then pray to Him, His word believe,
have faith and trust Him, come what may.

He'll do the rest, He'll lead us on
To where we all should be,
He'll help us, guide us, strengthen us,
Please ask him in, He's *real* for thee.

B Mills

THE MILLENNIUM

A public celebration of my Saviour's birth,
It's time the world should be aware
Of Jesus' special worth.
In olden times, long, long ago
He came unto His own,
He was rejected then, and now
It's happening again.

But living in the hearts of those
Who love the Saviour's name,
He'll fan the flame to show the world
It was for them He came.
He died for you, He died for me,
He died for one and all,
That all our sins might be forgiven
If we accept His call.

You'll feel the warmth of Jesus' love,
His guidance and His care,
His presence will go with you,
Be with you everywhere.
He'll take you through life's journey
And when this life is through,
You'll spend eternity with Him,
Oh yes, He died for you.

D M Spraggs

SPRING

Fair Lady Spring, dull winter's tired retreat
Uncovers thy fresh beauty to our gaze;
And thou dost rise, through ever-lengthening days,
From veils of mist in tatters round thy feet,
And modestly doth clothe thyself, to greet,
Wrapped in a green and gold ephemeral haze,
Thy worshippers, while paeans of songbird praise
Transport e'en sorrowing hearts to Paradise Street:
And thou art wooed by sun and gentle rain,
Who kiss the slumbering Earth awake, to bring
From wintry death, the flowers which form thy train,
And count thee fairest in their numbering.
We, too, shall wake from death, to live again
And blossom in an everlasting spring.

Mary Roberts

POWER THROUGH GOD

Daily prayers and kind thoughts always create a powerful force
Badly needed in times of distress, sorrow, grief or remorse.
Uplifting hymns of praise and anthems of joy help dispel strife
Religious ceremonies and rites guide our journey through life.

Practical aid for the troubled greater than ever today
Children, health and animal charities to which people pay.
Support a cause dear to your heart, see if friends will do the same
Remember what you approach on this earth is done in His name.

M E Beale

THAT HELPING HAND

I fall and stumble
But you pick me up,
Your love makes me feel humble.

You see beyond the human eye
Deep within our hearts,
That's why you are our God on high.

Though our ways be classed as sin,
Help is at hand,
You promise to change us from within.

To walk with You, our hand in Yours
Will keep us safe,
To cross life's dangerous highway through everlasting doors.

I'm no longer afraid and tremble,
Even in my darkest hour
Your angels gather and assemble.

To guide us through yet gently led
With our faith intact,
This promise the holy bible said.

You are here, there and everywhere,
I see you in all creation,
My safety valve released by prayer, all thoughts made bare.

My hand is small and yours, large
Mine slips its hold at times,
Thankfully I say in prayer you are the one in charge.

J Rendell

Are You Really Dead?

Everything is the same as before,
Your toys scattered everywhere,
Your name on the door
And yet there's something missing.
That my son is you.
Yet with all your things around me
I wonder, are you dead?

I remember the doctor saying
'I'm sorry, I did all I could,'
But when I kissed you for the last time,
Your body was still warm with life.
Mummy thought you were only sleeping,
At least she hoped this was true,
But suddenly it hit me,
Is he really dead?

Each Sunday morning up I get
And gather things together,
Then off I go to where you rest
And tenderly place each flower,
I feel you're right there with me,
Watching me, and that is why
I wonder, are you really dead?

My life is hell without you
I'm not allowed to cry,
I'm told I must forget you,
But if I do I'll die.
Others have forgotten you
But I'll forget you never,
When I can look at your photo,
I have to sigh and say,
My son, are you really dead?

Yes you're dead in a sense,
But my love for you lives on,
So really you are sleeping
Until it's time for me to come.
It's such a lovely though my pet
That soon we'll be as one.
Are you really dead my love?
No, you're only sleeping,
Waiting for Mummy to come.

A M Tully

MILLENNIUM PRAISE

Another thousand years of time
is coming to an end.
Two thousand, of the truth of Christ,
the message to the world we send,
the bells ring out to tell the worth
of the Saviour born on earth.
Candles burn, a Flame of Hope,
a light of Faith that burns within,
shines out to all, God's truth to bring.
Sweet incense rising from our praise
to glorify God's holy name,
to carry high for all our days,
the *truth*, the *light*, the *hope*, the *flame*.

Marlene Meilak

LINK - AGE

Steadfast love and hope
are together with us
when we place our faith in you.

The desire to operate
in your love,
and with your compassion.

Tender mercies
surround us, when we receive
something of the revelation

Of what it is to love God
and others alike.

Wayne Hudson

PUT YOUR HOPE IN GOD

Though my soul be disturbed
I'll put my hope in God
When I'm restless and confused
I'll put my hope in God
I know that I can trust Him
He enfolds me in His love,
I know He's always with me
His promises I trust.
Don't despair, oh my soul
Put your hope in God,
Don't be downcast, oh my soul
Put your hope in God.

Sandra Barton

CAMPANULA IN RAIN

Taking the shortest cut
the rain pelts down
in straight concerted drops
hitting the ground
and pummelling the weeds.

The Canterbury Bells
on slender stems
lean forward, bowing
to superior force,
but when the onslaught slackens
rise again, continue swaying,
nodding purple heads
like bells in thanks
to the much needed rain.

Mavis Scarles

GETHSEMANE

Alone in dark Gethsemane
Perspiring droplets of blood,
My Jesus knelt in agony
Whilst angels were sent from God.

In that garden He could have died,
But the timing was not right,
So the angels' strength was applied,
Holding Him in arms of might.

I kneel in my Gethsemane,
So afraid that I will die,
But the time is not right for me,
So strong angels to me fly.

Winifred Rickard

WITH OUR LIVES

In our autumn years
We can look back on
All the good times
As well as mistakes
All the wonderful memories
We've gathered through time
And recalled as if just yesterday
When the children were young
All the laughter
The fun we had simple
And good
As they grew they were taught
Faith the right way
For their journey through life
As we should
Now I see them
As grown men and women
They have principles, love
I'm so proud
With faith it has grown
And whatever they do
God will be with them throughout
It will grow and in time
Spread around us
With our lives
That is how it should be
With God at our right hand forever
It will give all the comfort we need

Jeanette Gaffney

CAST OUT INTO EXTERIOR DARKNESS

*(In 1989 spools of information relating to planet Earth were loaded on
a spacecraft which would in due time leave the solar system for the
depths of interstellar space)*

We sent from Earth our unknown message
To stars and moons and other planets.
Envisaging our flora, seas and fauna,
Will searchers seek, or will they ban it?

They'll hear our words, our winds, our waters,
And see our colours, clear and dappled,
Will they perceive in this creation
Belief in God, a church as chapel?

With pride we've recalled to those world afar
The slow sure march of mysterious Mammon.
Did we with equal pride remember
Christ's redeeming love, God's own dear Son?

Did we recapture the Bible stories
That show why the world is the way it is,
Of sorrow, sin of love of laughter,
Of self-sacrifice, beauty, eternal bliss?

Have we enthralled those far-flung listeners
Of only those things that went not wrong?
Or did we warn there's good and evil
Through; poems, hymns, sagas, songs?

If they are believers far away
And though we are we have not said,
Remembering Christ's last command
They will pass by - 'Yes, that one's dead.'

P Cockin

I WALK IN PEACE

I walk in peace, for Jesus walks beside me,
Spreading His loving blessing o'er each day;
Giving me strength when I am weak and helpless,
His benediction at the close of the day.

I walk in peace for I have His forgiveness,
Freeing my soul from every bond of sin;
Giving new life, a really new beginning
Cleansing my soul from every stain within.

Oh! This is why I love my blessed Saviour,
And this is why I long to play my part;
Oh! Jesus I am yours, now and forever,
Your love for me finds echoes in my heart.

W Herbert G Palfrey

THE MORNING PRAYER

I asked the Lord for patience
In the day that stretched ahead
And softly through the silence
I heard these few words said.

Be still and know that I am here
To comfort and to guide.
Never feel that you're alone
For I am by your side.

Grieve not when all the things you plan
Sometimes may go amiss.
Face the morning with a prayer
And you'll draw your strength from this.

P Lampard

THE ULTIMATE GOAL

I took a stroll to the hills one day,
Way up high and far, far away.
My heart was drawn to the closeness of God,
As I felt I was walking the steps he had trod.

I cannot explain the warmth and the love,
That swirled all around and within and above.
I forgot all my sorrows and worries and plight,
And soared like eagles with wings spread in flight.

I drifted way up far beyond earth's domains,
With angels in heaven and God, where he reigns.
There was singing and music and joyfulness there,
For the love of God's people and mankind to share.

If only it could be like this back on earth,
Just loving, not killing, for all that it's worth.
To reach out and touch your friends and your neighbours,
And then we could say, 'Here's the fruits of our labours.'

How pleased God would be with you and with me,
If He could stand back with joy and see
That we really are learning His works and His ways,
And endeavour to do so the rest of our days.

Peace be with you, for don't you see,
That God dwells within you,
And also in me.

C Kay

WHEN MY HEART SPEAKS

When my heart speaks, I put my pen to paper,
The words just seem to flow like swiftly running water,
I have so many questions that are needful of an answer.
What gives a bee its instinct?
Or gives perfume to a flower?

When I look at trees I have to realise
That from a tiny acorn grows a mighty oak of power.

If you have ever heard a lark upon the wing,
Don't you ever wonder where it learned to sing?
Should you answer it is nature, then nature must be God.
God was the bird's creator,
He created everything.

The concrete may clamber over each mile of countryside,
And cars befoul the air in increasing circles wide
In this ever-changing world, my pen I will always wield,
While I can still see a daisy growing wild upon a field.

Dorothy Leech

ASSISI

In a small Franciscan chapel
We pilgrims bow our heads in prayer,
While reverently the sunlight creeps
Along the polished floor and stair.

Far from the distant hills of Wales
We humbled few are gathered here
To honour and to praise the saints
Where trod Saint Francis and Saint Clare.

A rich, warm silence soaks the air
As bread and wine are served to all;
And then, as if to cast a spell,
The air wafts in a dove's soft call.

Meanwhile, outside on the wall
Good Francis might have gently smiled;
For he had spoken with the dove
And understood the call of love.

Reginald Massey

SANCTUARY

Away from the noisy city,
Away from the crowded street
To somewhere serene and peaceful,
To a place where the air smells sweet.
A peaceful spot where I may hear
The song of a bird on high
And feel the warmth of a golden sun
As it shines in a cloudless sky.
Where no buildings blot the landscape,
Or exhaust fumes foul the air,
Where only animals roam the fields
As they graze on the green grass there.
Here I could find contentment,
Free from worry, fear or care,
A valley steeped in silence,
A sanctuary rich and rare.

Graham S Hamilton

CHERISH EACH MOMENT

Endeavour not to live in the future - or the past,
Live for today the present, for undoubtedly it will last.
We know what has gone, we have no idea what will come
But for now, enjoy each and every moment, for that - do succumb.
The past is filled with memories, the future, who knows
        what it will bring,
Hopefully much happiness, contentment, problems gone,
       a new sense of spring.
To dwell on the past, think only of the good times, not sad
Then the present can be enjoyed, the future - strength - be glad.
All mortal beings at some time will receive peace of mind,
Strength and goodness, believe in the Almighty - these you'll find.
It was God's gift to each and every one of us,
So live for the present, the future then may be discussed.
The moral to this is our life is mapped out, not planned,
Maybe then one day we'll all be able to understand.
The past is gone, cannot be changed, present here and the future to come,
Keep this belief, then that day planned for us will - inevitably come.

Irene J Mooney

FOR HE IS IN HIS HEAVEN

Whether you're up, whether you're down
In with a crowd or out on your own
If you're looking for Jesus He will come your way
For He is in His Heaven every night and day

Bring in the harvest, bring in the hay
Say prayers for the sowers and reapers today
For blessings He has sent us, let Him hear us say
For He is in His Heaven every night and day

Seasons may come, seasons may go
Spring brings the baby lambs after the snow
Wondrous things are happening since Jesus came our way
For He is in His Heaven every night and day

Kingdoms may come, kingdoms may go,
The Devil has his palaces down below
But God is in His Heaven every night and day
His kingdom lasts forever He is here to stay

Barbara Tunstall

MILLENNIUM THOUGHTS

One thing is certain time never stands still,
It moves on relentless against our will.
Is it two thousand years since Christ was born?
A son to Mary on a Christmas morn.
His birth in a stable cold and bare,
A star foretold this event so rare.
Shepherds and wise men came to see
Offering their gifts on bended knee.
The world has moved on in every sphere.
The best we love, the worst we fear.
Have we really come so far from that stable
Bare and the wondrous star?
Through two thousand years your love conquers all,
Let us respond with our hearts when we hear the call,
To listen, and work for a far better world,
As the twenty-first century before us unfurls.

R Rowland

NOAH AND THE UNICORNS

I was told a story when I was young one day,
Why there are no unicorns to be found at play.

Long ago the earth became full of wicked men,
Noah was told to build an ark and he obeyed God then.
As Noah gathered the animals, the unicorns stood by,
Looking up as dark clouds gathered in the sky.
Already some great puddles are laying on the ground,
The unicorns are having fun - splashing all around.

They are making so much noise when Noah's voice calls out,
Ignoring Noah's warning, they just splash about,
So Noah went into the ark, the door was tightly shut,
Down from the hills and underground flooding waters gushed.
All the evil on the earth at that time washed away
And with it went the unicorns because they disobeyed.

So I've never found a unicorn in the places I have looked,
But I know that they are beautiful from the pictures in my book.

Dawn Parsons

BABE OF BETHLEHEM

He came for you and me and all mankind
Born in a lowly stall,
No other shelter did Mary and Joseph find
For Jesus, but a stable of straw.

Such a lowly birth had he
After they'd journeyed so far.
Ox and ass on bended knee,
Shepherds under the guiding star.

Gifts brought by wise men three,
The babe nestled in a manger of straw.
Mary and Joseph such wonder did see
As they gazed in reverential awe.

As we celebrate Christmas and gifts receive
May we recall that night of afar
And as in comfort, you lay down to sleep,
Recall the divine miracle under Bethlehem's star.

K House

COMES THE DAY

Comes the day of crucifixion,
Soon the day of man's rejection comes,
The day of Jesus dying,
Then the day of death defying,
First the cross of agony,
Nailed upon that Calvary's tree.
From his lips forgiveness came,
Called upon his father's name,
Gave his life for all man's sins
So that we eternity can win.
Darkness fell as Jesus died,
Lowly thieves on either side,
One believed God's holy word
To give all that we deserved.
As he closed his tired eyes,
Looked on high to heaven's skies,
Son of heaven, mortal man,
God of love since time began.

J Winwood

OUR WORLD

Our world is a wonderful place,
It's the people in it
That make it all worry and hate,
Some are kind and some are not
If they help anyone,
They count the cost,
What with pollution, we haven't a solution,
Global warming getting through, dear God what can we do?
Air's getting thinner
And fishes getting skinnier,
What if the sea dries up?
Weather's out of season,
people have asthma and bad breathing,
It's nearly summer and it's freezing.
There is violence and shooting,
Raping and looting
But still we can save our wonderful planet.
If we try very hard
To put back from where we take,
This will make our world a better place,
Be kind to our folks
The trawler men in their boats,
Help them when in trouble,
Don't burst this precious bubble
Save our wildlife and all life,
Plants, trees and weeds,
Do try hard,
Please, please, please.

Shirley Rowland

Bede's 'History Of The English Church And People' (731 AD)

He writes with such engaging warmth, it's difficult
To take offence at Mother Church's rock-sure claim
To know what's best: detractors argued to a standstill
Not by rake or stake, but by the prayers of martyrs
Going up in flames themselves; by miracles

Of saintly healing; by the rising star of intellect
Justified by faith, investing the Unutterable
With the magic of the risen Christ and issuing in
Mind-boggling feats: battling bishops panicking
Whole armies into bloodless flight with shouts of

'Alleluia'; calming fires and raging seas.
Famine, plague, the sweep of the destroying sword
Have no power to dismay; nor this people, dispirited,
Stripped of their imperial legions and left exposed
To their marauding neighbours - and themselves: Mother

Has the measure of them all and knows what's best.
It's all so clear to him from Jarrow's monastic heights
Fifty years before the longboats bit into
The beaches of Wessex and the Viking Terror began:
The Church holds Britain's future in her lap: survival

Depends upon the earnest of its quest for Christ.

David Donaldson

PAIN

Open are the sluice gates of pain,
I tumble through the seething flood.
Will I disappear down the drain,
Or at the end will I find God?

Oh yes He's here, oh yes, He's there,
When I'm numbed and blinded by pain,
And I've been brought to that place where
All my self-effort is in vain.

Then in His loving arms I'll rest
And cease my struggle and my strife,
Acknowledging His way is best
As I yield to Him my whole life.

Winifred Rickard

WHO'S TO BLAME!

Everybody blames me
When anything goes wrong
When anything goes missing
Or they can't hear their favourite song.

It wasn't me who was driving,
It wasn't me who dictated the way,
It wasn't me who missed the usual turn,
But it was my fault anyway.

So what's the point of saying
Stop and think of what you do!
When things aren't always going right,
It might be down to . . .you!

Sylvia Connor

COMPUTER WISE

The computer and I
Are getting very friendly
You can understand why
I try to the end.

The computer I have to say
Does try me hard
But at the end of the day
I have gone onward.

The computer has its game
Up to all 'tricks'
But I am not so lame
And actually enjoy the 'frolics.'

The computer is good company
Can keep one laughing
The latter lost to many
Which means everything.

The computer dashes its mark
All over the screen
But I take it as a lark
Although sometimes one could scream.

The computer makes me laugh so
Like company with someone
Gives me such a glow
Especially when I 'think' I've won.

The computer knows it's got me
As I cheerfully 'print' my piece
Then what do I see?
Well, it's enough to make you 'shriek'!

Josephine Foreman

WHERE DID I COME FROM?

Lord I've often wondered,
Who placed us on this earth?
Where did we come from?
Who gave us earthly birth?

My friend you are many things,
The very earth itself,
The many chemical elements,
That has become material wealth.

You are the dinosaurs,
That roamed throughout the land,
You are the oceans,
You are the desert and the sand.

You are the air, the water,
The sweet smell of dawn,
You are the warmth of the sun,
That greets the early morn.

All these things you are,
All these things you've been,
Minute particles of atoms,
Too small ever to be seen.

What goes around comes around,
Like a carousel of delight,
You are the moonbeams,
That brightens up the night.

You are all these things and more,
You are divine love and light,
A spirit of the universe,
Full of energy that burns so bright.

Put all these together,
My answer to you will be,
Open your eyes that are blinded,
The truth you will but see.

You have always been around,
For the Lord planned it that way,
So the answer to your question,
Will be given to you one day.

M G Bradshaw

MY SAVIOUR

On a cross
On a hill
On a dark, lonely day
My Saviour,
God's Son
Took my sins all away.

In a tomb,
In a garden for three days He lay
Then arose
All His foes
He had driven away.

Now ascended
With the Father
In heaven He reigns
We must be ready
And waiting,
For He's coming again.

Jackie Holland

WINTER DAWN IN THE WOOD

At first light it is cold and crisp,
Sparkles dance upon first ground, and
Dew on silver grass washes my feet
There is music in the air, yet I hear no sound.

I wander through the thicket, where
Branches on trees sway leafless and bare
Soft winds blow through a wintry spinney
Beneath me, snowdrops grow white and fair.

Sunlight reflects upon a rippling beck,
Snow clouds drift by without a care
A robin rests his wings, perching on a rock,
In pure and fragrant air.

Looking around, I see no one, but
The Lord is with me, amongst silent trees
I feel tranquillity, staring into a stream
And against my face, blows a cool and gentle breeze.

A Jackson

CRIES FOR HELP

Upon our darkest hour
The depression comes about
Feelings of hopelessness and despair
Our lives it does impair

Cries for help from within oneself
But no one hears these cries
Except for the voices inside one's head
So we feel best tucked up in a warm cosy bed

The doctors and nurses do their best
To prescribe pills when we feel so ill
But nothing can spare the thoughts and cares
That whirl about inside our hearts

Delusions come, delusions go
Lethargy too causes such woe
Sleepless nights and restless days
For our illness there's such a price to pay

Joy Sharp

PROTECTING ARMS

My friend came down and kissed your brow
Then whispered gently in your ear,
'Now close your eyes and go to sleep,
There's nothing left to fear.'

And as you slept he took your soul
Then held it gently in his arms
He held it closely to his heart
And kept it safely from all harm.

He took you to a special place
And shared with you his tender love,
And as you gazed upon his face
You saw the wonders of above.

Your trial over, breath restored
Your soul, revived to start anew
He gently kissed your sleeping face
Whilst sharing all that you'd been through.

Susan Stratford

THE BARN

The night was cold and it was snowing
And as I lay warm in my bed,
I thought I heard a baby crying,
Or was it just the wind a-sighing.
I closed my eyes but could not sleep for the
                              sound of crying.

So, from my bed I rose and quickly;
Warm clothes I donned, then to the door.
Outside the snow had fallen thickly.
My face and hands with cold were stinging.
I listened hard to hear again that mournful sound
                              the wind was bringing.

An old dark building I discover
And found it was an ancient barn.
Inside was lit by candles flickering,
Two figures huddle close, protecting
A tiny babe, whose cry I'd heard in the night
                              so disturbing.

I searched for signs of them next morning
And thought it all had been a dream.
My coat and shawl I soon discover,
The things I'd used to give them cover
Laid on the floor, a cross of straw from a
                              grateful mother.

Sue Groom

CAROLS BY CANDLELIGHT

Soft glows the light from candles hung aloft,
Dim lit the shadowed spaces in between,
Notes from the organ, plaintive, low, yet soft
Rise gently in the air, heard clearly, but unseen.
On whitened ledge and wall the holly hangs,
In pew and chair the congregation stay
Waiting awhile with conversation hum
The time to stand, to sing, and on their knees to pray.
Here comes the choir, close followed by their priest.
The stately pace brings people to their feet,
All voices stilled and silent.
Waiting for the feast, where they with friends and God
May haply meet.
Not unvoiced now, but tunefully we sing.
Organ and tongue are one.
With loud and happy praise we celebrate His birth,
Our King.
Together all in worship, our voices heavenward raised,
What joy He brought the night He came to earth,
Signed by a star and in a stable born.
All hope to man, and ease of pain.
No dearth of promise to a world forlorn.
And so we sing, all people gathered here,
For one brief hour our lives are freed from stress.
We pray, we ask, we know
Our God is near. Our hearts are full.
We know that we are blessed.

Irene Lee

UNTITLED

The black of nothingness,
Void of un-being,
Cloud of unknowing:
Darkness hid eternity.

Starlight
   Twilight
      Moonlight
         Daylight:
            The sun declares the dawn.

                        Volcanic light
                    Thunder light
                White light
            Atomic light
        Light from Light

'Let there be light:'
A fireball of light -
The universe was born.

Mary Hale

MARY AT THE CRIB

Long, slow smile of knowing,
Deep glow of inner light,
Wild joy overflowing,
Her boy her one delight.

Music, though it's silent,
Magic of one shared love,
Glory in this advent:
Now see God from above.

Gold light in the centre
Fills quite the sacred space;
Silence is her mentor,
Essence of higher grace.

Mother beams at offspring,
Mortal is glorified
By smile of her God-King,
Ever to man now tied.

Anne Sanderson

THE ONLY ONE

When the heart is oppressed and our spirit
Longs for freedom from sin and despair;
When within and without there are conflicts
And it seems as if no one would care.

Jesus came in our midst from His Glory,
Not despising the human estate,
He alone took upon Him our burden of sin
His appearing did not come too late.

Nor indeed was it just done 'in passing'
Ineffective to some degree,
But dictated by God's deep compassion,
Man's salvation to accomplish came He.

There's a cross lifted up on a hillside,
Where perfection submitted to shame,
There to flee in our soul's deepest anguish
Is effective, and never in vain;
For the one, who His life gave to save us,
Full redemption for us did obtain.

Georgina Atkinson

UNTITLED

Oh my love
come live with me
on this barren rock
above the sea
where strong winds blow
grey mist doth creep
sea spray jumps
and inside seeps.

Oh my love
come live with me
in this towering castle
amidst the sea
with its iron doors
and grey stone walls
where lost past shouts
through echoing halls.

Oh my love
come live with me
in this forsaken place
way out at sea
where rolling fog
hides distant boats
pink rose petals
and warm fur coats.

Oh my love
if you're near me
on this barren rock
I'd love the sea
where the sky is high
the air is clear
and life is lost
of want and fear.

Amanda Michelson

FROM HIGHLANDS TO LOWLANDS

The undulating land of the Highlands
Coloured gaily with purple heather
Stretching across the open moors
To the grassy mountains above
With cattle grazing in inclement weather.

The wind howls across the open plains
Whistling thro' the yellow gorse
While sheep and cattle continue their labours
With winter raiding its usual course.

Then springtime's behest of natural beauty
Brings the golden sun to the highest peak,
Looking steeply down to the grass so green,
Across the wide open spaces to the Lowland,
Where the wind's no longer strong, but weak.

Then summertime covers the hills and dales
With the gift of sound from nature's young,
Stirring the air with their tiny voices,
Playing with leaves mature and strong,
And across the hills a song is sung.

The singing comes from you know not where,
The accompanying pipes play on
while a brown, majestic golden eagle
On the rugged mountain stands,
For this is the place where he belongs.

These open spaces of moors and hills
From Highlands to lowlands thrive,
Nature's gifts of creative powers
Built up of mysteries by unseen hands,
Blessing the miracles that keep it alive.

Eileen Chamberlain

LIVING IN THE MOMENT

Live in the moment,
Make the most of every day,
And you will feel such joy
As you put the past away.

Bless each of your yesterdays,
Every moment that has gone,
Any mistakes are over
And not to be dwelt upon.

You can never know
What tomorrow will reveal,
Your appetite to see the menu
Will only spoil the meal!

God has planned each second
Of the day that lies ahead,
If you trust in Him completely
He will show you the path to tread.

Life is there for you to enjoy,
Don't waste the chance to live,
United with Christ in the moment,
What a gift He has to give!

Barbara Manning

HALF MOON

With what grace sky-clad Selene
Inclines her pale cheek to the sun!
The jewel at her breast
As she sinks in the west
Is Venus, goddess of love.

A Cohen

BE READY

Will you be ready when Jesus comes?
You . . . one of His holy ones.
It may be in the dead of night,
Or in the time of broad daylight.

All those many years ago,
Because He loved His children so,
God sent Jesus, His only Son
Teaching on earth 'til His work was done.

Once before He sent His only child,
Gentle Jesus meek and mild,
Until when a man, He died for us,
High on a hill, nailed to a cross.

How will you know that it is He?
Our Saviour who died at Calvary . . .
Who took away the sin of man,
Dwell upon it, if you can.

His hands and feet will bear the marks
Where nails pierced through flesh and bark.
A wound at His side will show
Where a soldier's sword dealt the blow.

Soon from the sky, a mighty host,
Father, Son and Holy Ghost,
He shall come back in all His glory,
To complete the bible story.

So, be ready to receive Him then,
As to this earth He will descend
To take His people on to glory,
To dwell with Him . . . so ends the story.

Barbara Forsyth

IMPAIRMENT + DISABILITY = HANDICAP

Being deaf or dumb
Being lame or blind
Is real and physical
Not a state of mind.

So pity the afflicted
And try to be kind
Because physical 'impairment'
Is very easy to find.

'Disability' does not come on cue
It can be the curse of anyone
It could be me
It could be you.

The role of handicapped
Can be anyone's lot
It depends on whose name
Comes out of the hat.

So please carry through life
This simple map
That impairment + disability
Equals physical handicap.

So thank your gods
You who are free
From impairment plus disability
You're not handicapped like me.

John Doyle

BIRTHDAY GREETINGS TO THE QUEEN MOTHER

Your birthday anniversary
We celebrate today,
It is a time of gladness
To praise and thank and pray,
May God give you his blessings
Of hope and joy and peace,
Good health and trust for ever,
And love that will not cease.

We thank you for your service
To people far and near,
And in the days of wartime
Gave comfort, hope and cheer,
Your ways are ever gracious
They come right from your heart,
And help us travel onwards
To play our humble part.

Your courage over problems
Shows us not to despair,
And tells us help is give
To those who ask in prayer.
So many happy wishes
To you, our dear Queen Mum,
You are a great example
To each and every one.

Daphne Harman Young

HOW DO WE TELL THEM THERE'S A HEAVEN?

Out in the world people are dying,
Children are hungry, children are crying,
How do we tell them you love them Lord?
How do we tell them you care?

When there's no food and they're hungry and cold,
Their loved ones are dead and there's no one to hold,
They're all alone with no one to care,
Help us to go and Your love to share.

How do we tell them there's a heaven?
How do we tell them there's a God?
How will they know that You love them Lord,
When they are hungry, cold and unloved?

They will only know if You tell them,
They will only know if You go,
Take my love to them and show them I care,
That I will always be there.

I love these children, I really care,
I see their suffering because I'm always there,
These children I love will have a place with me
In heaven above.

Pauline Willis

MY LOVELY GRACES

My lovely graces are three tall trees
which daily bring enchantment,
whether clothed soft silver green
or revealing all their symmetry,
with arching branches interlaced
making a fanned cathedral roof,
the gentle glow of calm and peace
these graceful trees inspire in me
has a constant measure unaffected
by a damp December or any other woe.

When I'm grieved or feel downcast
their strength consoles and comforts,
gives nourishment to me and food
and shelter for small wild creatures
and other inhabitants of the wood;
the richness of fallen leaves feeds
delicate woodland cyclamen, violets
and anemones, giving grateful pleasure
in this magic world within worlds
and always the generous arms upheld
to liberate, not grasp or seize.

Monica Redhead

THE CHESTNUT TREE

I shall buy me a cottage when I am old
A board outside would show it is sold,
I shall have the key,
And outside the gate a chestnut tree
Will spread out its branches to capture me.

When the year is in decline,
And the showy candles no longer shine,
The green prickly cases their promise will share
For bountiful harvest to those who are there.
The protecting cradle will crack like a smile
And a glimpse of its treasure is seen for a while.

Then loosed from their anchorage
They bombard the ground
And mahogany conkers are scattered around.
The children come running as soon as they land,
How shiny and smooth they feel to the hand.
I've got some in my pocket to turn and to feel,
It may be a dream, but now it is real!

Margo Mallett

MEMORIES

Looking backwards down the years,
I find regret for many things I've done;
The pain I've caused, the many tears,
Shed by my thoughtlessness.

Taking too much for granted,
Expecting always what I thought my due,
And, in return, the grateful thanks I gave
Were all too few.

How much could I have done,
To help repay in just a little part;
But now, alas! The only paying I can do,
Is from my heart.

It is too late and now I find,
I'm left alone with just my memories
Of all those little, unrewarded deeds,
Left as my legacy.

H R Cullen

TRANSCENDENCE

It was indeed a 'whistle-stop' tour,
And we glimpsed the docks through a real downpour.
Most people followed the sign: 'Tea Room.'
I clasped my hat, walked on through the gloom
The guide book lists many an 'Expo' to visit,
But one place, above all, has lifted my spirit.
Here, the reward for looking around -
The 'Mariners' Church' with a peace so profound.
I thought of the heroes we call 'Cockleshell'
Of tall ships and liners and of the *one* who could quell
Raging seas at a word. Suddenly
I sensed I must turn to see a window, most wondrous.
It held my view,
Stained-glass glory by craftsmen true.
A shaft of light then just made it seem
That *here* a *lighthouse* had cast a beam.
When by dark days we are so o'erwhelmed,
think of the Saviour, 'The light of the world.'

Beryl Mapperley

COUNTDOWN!

Dong! 12 - The Man of the millennium,
Dong! 11 - Is the creator of this earth.

Dong! 10 - The Man of the millennium,
Dong! 9 - Marked its start with His birth.

Dong! 8 - The Man of the millennium,
Dong! 7 - Was and is, since the world began.

Dong! 6 - Heralding the coming age,
    He is the Son of Man.

Dong! 5 - Yesterday, today and forever,
Dong! 4 - Eternity is in His hand.

Dong! 3 - Jesus, the Man of the millennium,
        The Man in whom I stand.
        Because . . .

Dong! 2 - The years of the millennium,
        Are but tiny grains of sand . . .

Dong! 1 - In eternity.

Julia Smith

IMMERSION

B - become
A - a new
P - person
T - take this
I - immersion
S - save your soul
M - make amends with the master.

Eve Hughes

To My Sons . . . (On Dreaming)

When we're young we often dream of what we'd like to be,
We dream of what the future holds and of our destiny.

'A famous pop-star' some might say would be their special dream,
Every time that you appeared, your frenzied fans would scream.

Then others dream of football, such longing deep within
To score that goal at Wembley, the FA Cup to win.

Perhaps to be an actor, by everyone adored,
At the final curtain, oh, how they would applaud.

'Olympic stardom' some may choose, dreaming of a gold,
On that winning podium, their joys would be untold.

Others hope to write good books, best sellers by the score,
Their fans would read them avidly, and still cry out for more.

'An astronaut,' now there's a dream, travelling to a star,
Shooting off to outer space, to planets near and far.

Some dream they'll own a business, bringing wealth untold,
To own a mansion and a yacht, wear rings of finest gold.

Some just want to fall in love, they dream of wedded bliss,
Of children and a happy home, they only long for this.

There are so many choices, decisions you must make,
You'll often feel confused, which pathway should you take?

So please think very carefully, before your dreams you spin,
But with foundations firm and sure, you're ready to begin.

Build your dreams upon a rock, right from the very start,
Fix your eyes on Jesus, ask Him into your heart.

My dearest child, I hope your dreams one day will all come true,
And pray that God will guide you in everything you do.

Pam Newborough

THE MILLENNIUM LEGACY FROM 1999

The guys and gals of World War Two
Have left a millennium legacy for you,
Their children's children, singers, actors,
Their technology, the lot,
The legacy from them is really 'hot',
Their handsome sons, daughters to pass on their beauty,
You may say, all the old soldiers really did their 'duty'
They knew the best of Hollywood,
Great music passed on for you,
Cared much for their comrades, and pretty girls too!
They showed what they were made of,
look what they left behind,
Those guys and gals of yesterday
No better legacy to find,
They've passed on all their assets,
For a great mankind,
Let the millennium welcome them in
From nineteen ninety-nine.

Lily May

GIVE GOD A CHANCE

When your heart is full of joy
Ask God to share it with you
To join in the happiness you feel
Then He will be happy too.

When the weight of sorrow drags you down
God wants to share in your tears and pain
He will support and lift you up
Remember He has suffered the same.

When it's just an ordinary day
Let Him be part of that too
Ask Him to use you to spread His love
He will surely bless all that you do.

Every single day of your life
Give God a chance to be near
He will always surround you with His love
So you will have naught to fear.

Margaret Baggott

REPENTANCE

Father forgive - when my thoughts are disloyal
to the One whose love is true.
Father forgive - when I forget to give thanks
for the wonderful things You do.
Help me, please, to be content when things go sometimes wrong.
Let Mother Nature be my mentor and teach me
to lift my voice in prayer and song -
to echo in green valleys midst the beauty You have wrought for me -
such gifts of fragrant flowers and fresh breezes from the sea.
Father forgive - when anger haunts me
and past 'hurts' invade my mind.
Let me know Thy understanding grace and leave sinful hate behind.
For there is no need for vengeance, only love can find the way -
to salvation and Your commendment
on the Final Judgement Day.

Mary Elizabeth Allan Poynton

CHURCH CANDLE, MOTH AND ME

Singed, speckled wings, magnetic moth drawn to the church
                                        candles' glow,
Spectrum stains, panes ordained, holiness hypnotic in snow.

Entombed in granite grey, a frozen frame stares with eyes transfixed,
Anaesthetising body bleeding stretched high on crucifix.
Carved chiselled saints in architrave iced, gaze in sympathy,
Demoralised, bedraggled speck have sympathy, it is me.
Save the soul of this chosen child that hangs her head to the ground,
My shivering tear-stained shell, so humble pleads but my voice
                                        makes no sound.

Jesus how I long to hold you close within these arms,
Kiss your brow so bruised and torn and shield you from all harm.
If I were a robin I would mop with my breast the tears of blood
                                        dripping down,
And pluck Satan's thorns one by one, gently from your crown.

Each thorn a pain that pricks my ragged conscience raw and bare,
Did we forsake you Jesus, is that why you hang helplessly there?
Blinded eyes cry tender tears, a leaded heart is breaking,
Lonely hands hold sombre shadows 'Lord have I been forsaken?'
Eerie prayers echo from my mouth, 'Mercy for one and all,'
Crepuscular ghosts slowly creep up on a crying, sobbing lost soul.

Faintly faith flickers low, in the church candles' glow where
                                        no one else can see,
In solitude two hearts are found, the little moth and me.

J Wiltshire

TIME WAS . . . TIME WILL BE NO MORE

No time for this, no time for that . . . scarce time for work or play:
So all the tasks still on the list must wait another day.
The pattern just repeats itself as day will follow day,
We should have our priorities in order, come what may.

So many have so little time they scarce know where to start:
The great Creator has it planned . . . eternity in man's heart.
Man must go faster, farther, higher: the mountains he must climb
But all the while the pressure's on . . . he's running out of time.

Created for eternity, apprenticed here in space;
Our boundary set here in time, recipients of God's grace.
We've failed to follow His commands, His word makes this quite clear,
Life here on earth's a training ground: eternity is near.

Eternal life, eternal death, the curtain will come down
For you and me the choice is set . . . separation or a crown.
The crown of life, eternal bliss, whatever that enshrines;
Eternal life to serve the God whose glory all out-shines.

We've all come short of God's set mark, and put self in His place,
But God came down to pay the debt, we're trophies of His grace.
The new millennium looms ahead, 'twill be with us 'ere long:
Whilst here we're running out of time, it's there that we belong.

There where the clamping grip of time and space restrict no more.
There, where the host of God's redeemed will serve for ever more.
There is still time as we read this, the midnight hour will chime:
So, let's now face the simple truth . . . we're running out of time.

R Carnell

TWO THOUSAND YEARS

We did not see the Infant King,
We did not hear the angels sing,
Two thousand years ago.

We did not hear the angel say,
'Fear not, I bring good news today.'
Two thousand years ago.

We did not see the guiding star,
We did not meet the kings from far.
Two thousand years ago.

Yet we know well the Christmas song,
The guiding star to all belong.
Two thousand years today.

We offer gifts of praise and love,
To Christ our king in heav'n above.
Two thousand years today.

We celebrate the Saviour's birth,
Let songs of joy ascend from Earth.
Two thousand years today.

M Lacey

MY GARDEN

My garden's not a showpiece, with beds and borders grand
And I haven't got a 'treasure' coming in to work the land.
Sometimes it gets neglected, there's so much else that I must do,
But still the tiny seeds survive and keep on pushing through.
I've little time for watering, or hoeing to and fro -
And often really wonder where all the day's hours go!
A favourite spot I keep though, in memory of a dear and faithful pet,
It's full of pansies and Forget-me-nots - his spirit's with me yet.
I love the scented roses, orange marigolds - lilies tall and white,
The tubs of red geraniums, lobelia and fuchsia blooms so bright,
But when the grass is getting long, it's still pleasing to my eye
To find the many so-called weeds when I am passing by.
Celandines, pink daisies, clover, minor bindweed too -
Hawksbeard, golden trefoil and the dainty speedwell blue.
I really do feel sorry, when need drives to get the mower out
And I have to cut off all their heads and see them lie about!
Once more the lawns are tidy, but it does seem quite a shame,
Then I can hardly wait, until they all grow back again!
The Lord made all plants beautiful, so I wonder who decreed
Which flowers would be most welcome, and all others classed
                                                    as weeds!

Kathleen Stokes

ALPHA AND OMEGA

Alpha, Omega, the beginning and the end,
The creator of the universe is born to men.
Eyes that see beyond time and space
Look with love upon a mother's face.
Shepherds and wise men are invited to see
The birth of hope for humanity.

Alpha, Omega, the beginning and the end,
The author of life walks with men.
Hands that sculptured creation's form
With compassion reach out and touch the forlorn.
The blind, the hopeless, the desperate, the weak
Find healing virtue in the Messiah they seek.

Alpha, Omega, the beginning and the end,
The creator of eternity dies for men.
The voice that transformed creation's dark night
Cries out in anguish for man's sinful plight.
His body broken, disfigured and maimed
As he pays for man's freedom with suffering, with pain.

Alpha, Omega, the beginning and the end,
The light of the world has risen again.
Eyes that see beyond time and space
Look upon our lives with compassion and grace.
The cry of his heart is 'Come unto me
And I will take your burdens and set you free.'

K J Hooper

STARS OF BURMA AND BETHLEHEM

Midnight, just a breath from a tomorrow.
Tomorrow, a day that cannot really be.
If only time was something I could borrow,
To take and use to make people see
The wasteful thoughts, that look back to a time
Called yesterday, when all seemed perfect in their memory.

Midnight, suspended betwixt and between
The day ended, gone, and a future beckoning.
Times past, but not lost upon a memory evergreen
Of the way people were, by my reckoning.
With dreams of a tomorrow where mankind
Could forward look to an unknown day to come.

Tomorrow, mentioned on a hill far away
By unselfish heroes of a war scarcely won.
'For your tomorrow we gave our today,'
Reads the message they left upon tablet of stone,
To record and retain in our memory
Their dying for us in a far eastern land.

One other is worthy of our looking back
To times of warfare upon the earth.
'For your tomorrow' should read the plaque
In memory of Him, who gives us second birth.
He gave His 'today' that we may embrace
Tomorrow, a future that looks heavenward.

S Herbert

A FRESH START

Five . . . Four . . . Three . . . Two . . . One
The final countdown to the millennium;
As party-goers reach hysteria,
Nature silently enters a new era.

Now the streets are subdued and still,
But evidence of the party remains.
Everybody now has had their fill,
And soon life will return to the norm and mundane.

There have been years of preparation;
A sense of wiping the slate clean,
Everyone has been waiting with anticipation
But Y2K disruption remains to be seen.

To learn from mistakes and make a fresh start
Is what everyone is talking about;
To look at within and search your heart.
Use this opportunity to sort your life out.

Who or what is the God of your life?
And does that satisfy your soul?
Perhaps now is the time for you to decide,
And to gain a feeling of being made whole.

2000 years may have gone by,
Since Jesus hung on a cross to die,
But His love for you is why He came
And His saving grace is still the same.

Patricia Ann Ward

I'VE BEEN CHOSEN

I've been chosen
As a ball of shapeless clay
To be moulded into a vessel
To be used day by day.

Maybe I'll be a jug
Just to pour out to others, God's love
Of what it cost to send His son
Who descended from above.

Maybe I'll be a vase
To display what God has made
you didn't have to come
But your Father's will you obeyed.

Maybe I'll just be me
To serve Him like God has planned,
To be a servant of the Lord
To witness throughout the land.

Help me Lord, to learn how to serve
And not just to be a pea in pod
A unique and moulded vessel
Chosen by the true and living God.

Robin Woolgar

SACRED NIGHT

Born in a stable, in a manger he lay
Cosy and warm in a nest of hay.
Mary and Joseph proudly looked on
With love and wonder, their special son.
Shepherds received the news with joy,
They hurried to Bethlehem, seeking the boy,
Wise men came from afar
Bringing gifts, gold, frankincense and myrrh,
Kneeling they worshipped the baby small
Cradled in a manger, in an oxen stall.
Praises sing, let your hearts be light
For Jesus Christ, hope of the world,
Was born that sacred night.

Audrey Myers

HOPE

The trees are bare, the earth is dark and still,
No flowers bloom, no busy songbirds trill,
The earth seems empty, dead and desolate
How long till winter ends must we await?
But on a barren tree, a spider's web
Sprinkled with dewdrops, swings above my head.
Like twinkling stars lighting up the way
Towards the promise of a brighter day
While 'neath a hedge a tiny flash of white
A little snowdrop, which has won the fight
One more, to pierce the barren, sullen earth,
And bring the hope of spring again to birth.

Kathleen M Woodford

SOMETIMES

Sometimes Lord when I feel a little low
and tears not far away,
I simply set my mind on you,
just close my eyes and pray.
And oh I'm lifted by your grace
and moved by love,
sustained and cherished in your care.
Just knowing Lord I have a special place,
that where I am, you surely must be there.
I thank you Lord for love, for grace . . .
All crucified . . . Your precious gift!
That all your children should be free.
For I was given life . . . the day you died.
You rose!
And made a path to Heaven just for me.

M Marklew

ST PATRICK'S CATHEDRAL, NEW YORK

A new world symphony
Cast in sacred stone
Echoes around
Mid Manhatten's
Glitzy ghettos
Showering hope
Over a bright-eyed
Metropolis
Mesmerised by
Hologrammed highglass
Never-ending neon
And touchy tycoons
Trapped in tinsel towers.

James Adams

GOOD FRIDAY JOHN'S STORY

As I stood at Peter's side he said 'I love you Lord
I will do all you may ask even be put to the sword.'
Jesus' eyes grew very sad as he looked into Peter's face
'My rock you will deny me thrice before the cock crows day break.'
Peter said it will never be I will always be by your side
Then Jesus said 'I must leave you, the time has come for me to die.'
The soldiers came and took my Lord, I followed as close as could be
Into the courts of the Pharisee's where lies said he would not go free
Tho beaten and bound my Lord stood tall
Then they marched him to stand before pilate
A radiance shone around his form serenity in his silence
With pride and fear I followed on to the hill and his terrible death
I stood with Mary and held her hand as Jesus paid our debt
I watched his face and prayed to God, 'Please Father set him free
Jesus' eyes and ours then met, he said 'Mary listen to me
I leave you John as your son, My Father is waiting you see.'
Jesus then closed his eyes with forgiveness on his lips
The sky grew dark, the thunder roared, the temple curtain ripped
I, John will keep my promise until my life is done
I will care for Mary, the mother of God's son.

Gillian Mullett

THE MILLENNIUM DEBATE

Mervyn holds court, intellectuals give forth.
Will Christianity survive? Hope is diminished,
all agree - but one.
The debate goes on - all seem confused,
the Bishop recants - maybe God will survive the millennium.

Orthodox, Catholic, Liberal, Evangelical all join the debate.
Academics spar, Professors and Bishops lock horns,
Will a consensus emerge?
'He's real to me,' said one:
ignored, they rant but it's not yet rage.

Millions view and listen will Christ emerge
what shape will He take?
Discredited Christians what do they believe
slavery, female priests, war - what next?
The debate builds and a voice cries,
Enough! 'Don't you care my son died!'

Heads turn in dismay - Who interrupted our debate?
Viewers' ears awake - what is this?
Mervyn calls for resumption, the debate resumes.
The viewer sleeps but a man appears with nail pierced hands and feet;
how dare he in interrupt our debate!

Greg Walton

THE WORLD IS WAITING

Children's faces radiantly glow amid snow drifts and mistletoe, crinkly
Holly and Yuletide fires, bells pealing from old church spires.
Carol singers with voices shrill proclaiming the season of goodwill.
Street musicians huddle together for warmth against the biting weather.
Elderly shoppers with unsteady feet queue at butchers for last
Minute meat, handkerchiefs dabbing at watering eyes - anxiously
Glancing at snow filled skies.
A chirpy robin on a snowman's hat keeps a wary eye on a passing
Cat - but this bird's nobodies Christmas fare, a flip of a wing
and it's safe in the air.
Clanking shovels of folk chipping ice, sweet aroma of mince
Pies and spice. Flickering candle and frosted panes, fairy lights
Dancing on candy canes.
Merry laughter from a crowded inn as they gather together
Friends and kin, raising glasses of frothing ale - sturdy brew
not for the frail.
And so it was long, long ago, when a woman with child had
Nowhere to go. The inn was full - no room at all - so her
baby was born in a humble stall.
When in the midst of Christmas cheer remember that devine
mystical year - recall who's birthday you're celebrating, He'll
come again - the world is waiting.

R Holmes

THIS CAN'T GO ON

This can't go on - waiting all alone
That gate ajar - no need to phone
It's just a waste of time, of space
Here I am; wrong time, right place

A sucker for that holy charm
How can I stay so cool, so calm?
Surely soon something will crack
Patience that I do not lack

I hope she's fine, no calls been made
When all this time, the price she paid
No deja vu could I just bear
This empty heart she will but snare

Another one lost to fly away
Maybe soon someone will stay?
But why with me? A hopeless fool
So wicked and so wildly cruel

I'm going now, I've had enough
So hard they think, but not so tough
Don't worry now for I'll be fine
My only friend is left to pine.

Paul Davis

BLUES BRIDGE

I cannot achieve perfection
Or live life like a clown
I may wear this painted smile -
But it doesn't stop me feeling down.
My skin is enveloped in clay
This face mask is peeling and
My pores are grey.
To sink this low wasn't my intention
Best leave this cleansing routine for another sensation.

We're all standing on the Blues Bridge
Water laps up on every side
We try to escape but are trapped by the tide.
Reflections are wrinkled, ripples are splintered
Time is in shock - the season is winter.
A people of talent, a people of force
Imagination, destruction, decay and divorce:
We've built ourselves a Blues Bridge.

We drag ourselves to parties, go out drinking every night;
Smoke drugs? Hey, let me ask you just
How high's your kite?
Rockets fly out into space
Nature's decaying to humour the human race.

We're all standing on the Blues Bridge
We've built ourselves a Blues Bridge
Marching on a Blues Bridge
No toll to pay - only misery is found
Feet firmly on the ground, on the Blues Bridge
Built ourselves a Blues Bridge.

Kerryanne Delbridge

THE WISE MEN

Long, long ago on a cold winter's night
When all the stars were shining bright,
There rose in the east, a beautiful star
It outshone the others, was brighter by far.

There were in those countries very far,
Three wise men who saw the star.
It said in their books the star would bring
News of the birth of a very great King.

So they journeyed a long, long way
They rode by night and slept by day,
They came to Jerusalem where Herod the King
Was asked about this marvellous thing.

But Herod knew not and asked his seers
In Bethlehem the prophets tell us.
Then Herod told the wise men to go
And find the babe so he could come too.

The wise men went and the star still led them
Right over the town of Bethlehem.
They found the babe lying in a stall
He was so helpless, sweet and small.

The wise men knelt in His presence
And offered their gifts of gold, myrrh and frankincense
Then they returned home another way
And Mary remembered what they had to say.

E Spick

CHRISTMAS

'Give my son, to that human saddened place
Called earth . . . ?
And let them
Treat Him to Death?'

And yet, and yet He shall reign
In the hearts of many
For such
A noble gesture

And for this, we celebrate Christmas
With tinsel and lights
And overwrought nerves
We human beings

Christmas.
Christ, the child amongst ragged shepherds;
Three men wiser, after following
An abstract Christ, seriously

He comes with no package
No big deal: No January sale
Only the gentle music of the King Singers
And a hopeful look in his eye.

Andy McMaster

WHO IS OUR GOD AND LORD?

Fallen idols rise up again
Gilded in alluring new disguises,
Demanding more burnt offerings
And bigger sacrifices,
Promising paradise now
By conforming to every day attitudes
And tinsel platitudes.

Our weak knees tremble with desire
To bend, worship and give in,
Deceived by hearts lonely,
  Craving for power and signs,
  By minds making castles in the air,
  By feet trampling the earth
  Of your terrestrial birth.

You do not demand burnt offerings
Nor do you promise an instant paradise.
To love us into being, you tread tenderly our earth
And invite us to do the same,
To knit the memory of you
Into our living
To the glory of your name.

Angela Matheson

GOD KNOWS

I am who I am, in this world today,
Created by God's own hand,
He moulded me and shaped me,
Hoping I would understand,
That to follow in his footsteps,
A better person I would be,
And to follow him down the road of life,
Great glory I would see.

God knows what trials await me,
In my life right here on earth,
He has known what was before me,
From the moment of my birth,
But to see me through this life on earth,
I must trust in the Lord above,
And he'll see me through my daily trials,
By protecting me with love.

Marjory Davidson

GOD'S PORTION

Whey ask for such a small portion,
When Jesus can give you all?
Why settle for scrap ends and rejects
When His best, He offers for free?

No man He has offered a pittance,
But more than enough and some spare,
Just ask, receive and accept it,
To each is allotted their share.

Your needs He will meet in abundance,
Pressed down, and overflowing the brim
It's just a matter of asking,
And putting your faith in Him

Why claim such a big God then ask him,
For such trivial meagre amounts
Think big, ask for double and threefold,
His giving will never run out.

Jeff Slack

TOTAL ECLIPSE

Like that poor shadow that passed for riches,
His uneventful blankness all amazed;
His looming stealth felt like spell of witches,
Humble and dark glowed in the brightness razed;

And as he sped, empowered mystery
Over lands unimpeded smooth as Class,
Enacted his role in human history
The emphasis borne on his simple pass;

Had blocked the sun's effulgent majesty!
In terms no plainer could be thus expressed
Of daylight and night made a travesty,
A diamond ring set for his parting jest!

So I think of the state of fame on earth:
The total eclipse of man's greater worth!

R Ashby

THE GREAT PREACHERS

It must be three decades before the millennium
Since most congregations heard
Their really outstanding preachers.
How we looked forward to the long booked visits
Of those ministers and laymen,
Few in numbers but gifted.

They would announce their texts -
Some of them most unusual -
And would wring all possible out of them.

Avoiding the tedious or hackneyed,
They would preach with power, zeal, thoroughness,
And could hold their listeners' attention
Perhaps for forty minutes.

Where are such preachers now,
Those through whom God might speak:
Preachers who would challenge us,
And sometimes change our lives?

Dora Hawkins

BRIDGE OF LIGHT

Across these worlds between us
In this world, which is our fate,
We have spun a slender bridge
Across, with a loving golden gate.

And as this bridge swings in the wind
With shadows of our doubts,
Unsure, as in its centre the
Threads are weakest yet.

How can we mend these delicate parts
That hold us together as one,
When we walk across the golden bridge
Into the light of the heavenly sun.

These works we do, in service for
Our fellow brothers of the light,
The chains of doubt fall off now,
The centre, strong and bright.

Kathleen Tupper

PUTTING BACK THE CLOCK

Time does not stand still,
A cliché so old, we sigh to hear again
And think of hurrying footsteps
Sweeping the years as with a broom
And hopes lie fallow;
Dreams are just sweet dreams.

Anachronism is the word
For turning back the clock.
That was the time - this is the time;
Just a space for thought or smile or tear
Amidst the pilgrimage of life
Forever fraught with motion.

If in truth we could turn back
The clock of time,
What would it avail?
Would we not still tread self-centred paths
And feel the world owed us a crown?
One life - one chance - that is the sure reality.

Myfanwy

SING A SONG

Sing of song of happiness,
A melody of joy,
Of baby's birth and children's mirth,
Of parent's love for girl and boy,
Of lengthy days and summer sun
And holidays we've just begun.
Of sand and sea and little boats
Where we can spend our day
Collecting shells where seaweed floats
And watch the seagulls in the bay.

Sing a song of rainbows
Where joys are tinged a-while
With little showers of rainy hours
And the sunlight hides its smile.
When troubles come as come they will,
We find the sun is shining still
Above, within the arch's hue,
Delighting all within it's sphere
And colouring the distant view
Until the rain clouds disappear.

Sing a song of thankfulness
For happy days and sad,
When there is pain, or loss or gain,
For good times and for bad,
For peace and love, for youth and age,
For life's book as we turn each page,
For knowledge gained and triumphs won
Within our earthly span,
For Heaven's pathway, here begun
And God's eternal plan.

Jean Duckworth

I PRAY A SPECIAL PRAYER

I pray a special prayer,
A special prayer, that you are there to guide me.
I dream a special dream,
A special dream, that you are there beside me,
Beside me as you guide me
through the mysteries and wonders of each living day,
Beside me as you guide me
through the trials and tribulations, then again I pray,

And as I pray,

I pray and in my prayer,
I pray that you will always be forgiving.
I dream and in my dream,
I dream you tell me life is there for living,
So live it to its fullest
and fill it to the best of your ability,
So live it to its fullest
and through it be the person that you want to be,

And then you say to me,

I hear you as you pray,
You pray a prayer and I will always hear you,
I'm with you when you dream,
Your dreams will tell you I am always near you,
I'm near you through each moment,
every minute, every second of your life until eternity,
I'm with you every moment,
till the time is right when I will bring you here to me.

Then all is very clear,
You are so near to me.

I pray a special prayer
and you are there.

Jim Sargant

MARY MAGDALENE

I can tell by your eyes . . .
That you have been hurt
many times.
Your sweet kisses
I implore, before
I go into battle.

She smiled her disdain,
And I was sometime
her dejected slave
Patience all languorous,
Pain, any amount of it,
The Holy Mother lies
In Whitnash Churchyard,
And I make up lines to my God
In Kate's meetings.

The mickey taker tests me
from of old.
Jesus said 'Turn the other cheek,'
O Karate, life and soul of Zen,
Teach me your way.

And now, all the wars
that have ever been,
Catch me as Christ without a cause,
Save that of knowing
I do your will.

You are every woman
I ever met.
Transubstantiate four,
You have been with me since
the fall of man
As Sarah, Ruth, as
Ex-prostitute Mary Magdalene.

And now as God the Holy Spirit
Sweet woman, give me the
right to kiss you tenderly,
And call you wife,
Under green leaves and starry skies.

Richard O'Shaughnessy

NOVEMBER SUN

Oh Lord, this bright day,
Brighter for coming after the dismal rain
Of past days, the clinging mist.
Now all is radiance,
And in the bushes the birds twitter and call,
Tiny long-tailed creatures, feathered darts
Flung across the sky
That flames towards sunset.
Behind now are the heavy clouds
And the sun throws the trees against them,
Brilliant red, or pale gold feathers,
Autumn's last defiance.
The bare ash trees droop fingers
Reflectingly in the spinney's pool;
Great trees tower above their own images,
While below the still water, the stream tumbles
In its headlong rush over the weir.
Move, move, for winter is upon us,
The colour will be gone, the sun
Once more clouded.
Here, in this rush of brightness,
Is the brave challenge to the encroaching shadows -
These last moments before the dark.

Sara Serpell

AFTER THE STORM AT THE ABBEY

The natural world around us
New . . . and clean,
Washed by God's purifying tears,
Tears sent to cleanse . . . refresh . . . renew
Our sense of wonder in His creation.

Towering Abbey walls, washed and gleaming,
Delicate . . . softened colours
Visible through the porous wetness
Of the ancient mellowed stone.

Raindrops dripping from glistening trees,
Glinting like jewels caught in the sunlight
Pushing its way through ragged rents
In angry . . . windswept clouds.

Glossy colour-enhanced petals
Throwing watery reflections
Into rippling . . . shimmering puddles,
Their impressionistic colours dancing
And merging with our own blurry images
As we gaze in undisguised wonder.

What joy to witness this manifestation . . .
This demonstration . . . this expression
Of God's power
In nature!

Janet Reeve

THE PRAYER OF A CHRISTIAN WITNESS

May I be a city
Set upon a hill,
Never to be hidden
Ready for Your will.
Lord, I'm deeply conscious
Of the power of sin;
Wash me in Your blood, Lord,
Put Your power within.

May I be a beacon
Throwing out Your light
In this world of darkness,
Giving folk fresh sight.
Keep it every shining
So that men will see
That You want to give them
Peace and harmony.

May my life bring honour
To Your name most high,
For my Heavenly Father
I would glorify.
Purify my body
To the uttermost,
For it is the temple
Of the Holy Ghost.

Andrew Walker

ONE TRUE FRIEND

When I'm scared and don't know what to do,
I always turn around and think of you,
I've not known you for long,
But you bring out in me a song.

You make me happy when I'm sad,
And calm me down when I'm mad,
You're always there when I am down,
And place upon my head a crown.

To make me special in my heart,
which lets me begin from the start,
You will always be there,
And always be fair.

No matter how bad I am,
You'll always stay calm,
And never leave my side,
Or let me crawl away and hide.

For you'll believe in me,
And will let me be free,
So long as I believe,
And do not deceive.

Leeanne Sarah Harrison

BELIEF

Who said that Moses spoke to God upon the mountain tall?
Who saw the loaves and fishes be enough to feed them all?
Who said He made the lame to walk, and made the blind to see?
Who said He paid the price for all the sins of you and me?
Can anyone come up to me and tell me they were there
Upon the hill with all the rest, they also stood to stare?
My whole life through I wondered what answers there would be.
But I had to wait until I died this God of yours to see.
The pearly gates of Heaven, are now before my eyes.
And as I walk towards them, I come to realise
I do not know will I go in? Only time will tell
For if I am refused then I must surely go to Hell!
And then a voice so loud rang out and it was full of love,
I knew in no uncertain terms it came from up above.
I had a friend just like you once - and Thomas was his name,
Even though he doubted me - I loved him just the same!
It was for someone such as you - I suffered and I died.
So don't be shy - please come on in - the gates are open wide.
You can believe just what I say - because I am the one.
You have been searching all your life, I am His only Son.

Letitia Snow

YOU HAVE A FATHER

You have a Father, He's creator and Lord.
Who sent prophets of old, who's Son is the word.
You have a father, you worship in song.
Omniscient and Holy, eternal and strong.

You have a father, who helps you each day.
To walk in the light, and shows you the way.
You have a Father, that keeps you from harm.
Whose moon rules the night, whose sun keeps you warm.

You have a Father, what ere may betide.
Though you go astray, who'll still be your guide.
You have a Father, by night and by day.
Surrounds you with angels, that keep Satan at bay.

You have a Father who teaches you lots.
Rebukes and reproves, saves you out of tight spots.
You have a Father who wants you to know.
The world needs a saviour and tells you to go!

You have a Father, whose Son came to earth.
Paid the price of your sin, and knows what you're worth
You have a Father who made all creation.
Who loves the whole world every tribe, every nation.

You have a Father who knows every sparrow.
You must serve every day, cos you don't have tomorrow
You have a Father, whose word is the light
A lamp for the path, and strength for the fight.

So you serve your Father, every day, every hour.
For He in His word provides you with power.
To triumph and win over Satan and Sin.
To hear at the last 'My child enter in.'

Snikpohd

HARVEST TIME

Great trees standing tall and proud
The hillside brown and bare
Tall green covering, no longer there
Now only dead roots strewn around
Some would say death is here

Many the uses for the trees
Good strong timber for our needs
Homes, tables and chairs
The ground has to be cleared
Harvest time is here

The ground has to be prepared
New seed to be sown
Watered by God's good rain
Warmed by God's bright sun
Green trees to grow tall and proud
Ready to be used again

Can we apply this to you and me?
The ground has to be prepared
Good seed to be sown
Nurtured by God's own Son
Watered by His Holy Word
Bring new life to some

Through the good times
Through the bad
Can we be fertile land
Washed by the precious blood
Watered by the life-giving Word
Harvested by a Holy Hand
To be His example in our land

Sheena Jack

A Child's Dilemma
(After reading about a child abused by its parents)

How can they know you as *Father*
When their own abuses them so?
Or trust the hands of compassion
When others bruise with each blow?

How can they think of Heaven
As a refuge, peaceful and calm
When their home is a prison of torture
Where they cower, fearful of harm?

Can they forgive the molester
Who teaches that evil is right?
How can they turn from the poison
Which stalks in the day and the night?

J Skinner

You Calm The Storm

Throughout the dark and dreadful night
When strength has gone, when I can't fight,
Lord Jesus I can see Your light
You come, you calm the storm

With sunrise comes another day
Just like a sheep yet I will stray,
I cry my Lord, you show the way
You come, you calm the storm

You are The Shepherd, I the sheep
You constantly my soul will keep,
When I awake or when I sleep,
You come, you calm the storm.

Elizabeth Hughes

WISHES

Were I granted a few wishes
And could hang them on a tree,
Firstly, I would wish for wisdom,
Patience and serenity.

Secondly, I would be asking
For good health and strength each day,
So that I might succour others
As they struggle on life's way.

Above all, I would be wishing
For a blessing from above
To unite the whole creation
In goodwill and peace and love.

H Royle Edwards

SHIFT WORK

The setting sun called to the moon
At the far side of the sky,
'My day is done, it's time to go,
I bid you now goodbye'.

The moon replied, 'Farewell my friend,
I'll spread my midnight awning,
And guard the land 'til you return,
God speed until the morning!'

And thus it is that sun and moon
Both bring their special gifts,
Maintaining watch around the clock
By working different shifts.

Lorna Pearson

LORD BREATHE IN US

Lord breathe in us the breath of life,
Give us the strength to conquer strife.
Your Holy Spirit stir our will,
So every task for you fulfil.

Enthuse our being with your love,
And warm our hearts as from above.
Arouse and motivate us now
To do your will - our favourite vow.

Oh be with us at work and play,
At home or school throughout each day.
Remove the strain and stress we bear,
Convert us to your child of care.

Encourage us to work for you.
Rid us of hate, corruption too.
Discrimination, jealousy,
No longer part of life in me.

O spread your influence round the world,
O Holy Spirit be unfurled.
May all the peoples of each land
Share equal bounty from your hand.

Oh Holy Spirit, source of power,
Fill our whole being hour by hour.
Help us to spread Your Gospel true,
Courageous in this task for You.

Michael Salmon

AN OLD FRIEND

The smell of freshly cut grass
Wafts over the garden fences.
Eyes close to welcome the guest -
An intoxicator of the senses.

Nostalgia removes mind from body
As his drug releases time.
We fly together in nature's melody
As I smell the beauty of His rhyme.

He comes to me bearing gifts,
Of childhood memories and fairy tale myths.
We build a bird's nest in the grass
And pray for more time in the past.

He stays with me until suffocation,
And then I can no longer sense more.
My eyes open in desperation,
For I cannot see His open door.

He leaves me by the roadside,
Smelling the fumes in strife,
But he cannot leave me inside
As my memory holds His life.

C Cole

HYMN 2000

Come! Explode with jubilation!
Glory! Glory! Shout your praise.
Music soars in our declaration,
For goodness none can erase.
Jesus Christ is our Saviour,
Past and present testify.
The future seals his vindication,
Worship rises to the sky.

Two thousand years with your favour,
Lightening our dark, dark world.
Cleaning rot and adding flavour,
Your kingdom grows with love unfurled.
Come and bring your adoration,
Jesus, everlasting Lord.
Glory to Him in our generation.
Give Him more than you can afford.

No calendars in eternity,
No buffers where we finish.
No fears in God's prosperity,
His love will not diminish.
Truth, justice and beauty combine;
Righteousness free to flourish.
Fellowship full to his design,
Precious souls He will nourish.

History whispered your story,
But in time the truth will swell.
Future perfected will shout your glory
Prophecy heard since Adam fell.
Jesus, wondrous, Holy Lord,
All honour to your great worth.
Power more than we can imagine
Celebrated since your birth.

Laila Lacey

WEEKEND BREAKAWAY

Choose to spend one hour in church
To close the week and start again.
Brief is that special interlude
Away from work; indulgence; strain
Apart from news and noise and rush
Where there is peace
To pledge a fresh beginning.

On entering say your private prayer
Thank God you're fit enough
To keep the weekly habit
Bless your dear ones. Remember those you've lost
Then face the alter with candles lit
And shepherd window giving lesson clear
Hope for a new beginning.

To kneel is humble. To pray unites
Friends and strangers on equal ground
Psalms, parables, commandments, hymns
Then take wine and bread beneath the cross.
There is no division found
Twixt rich and poor: Twixt old and young
It binds our new beginning.

Perhaps two or three are gathered there
But it is fine when many more
Fill the church at Easter; Harvest; Christmas time
Or pack it by collecting friends
To hear the marriage vows:
Or round the font, a babe to bless:
Or throng to honour one whose life has closed
Then we must help the saddened ones
Make a new beginning.

J Wood

ONLY THE START

Two thousand years have come and gone
Since, to this earth, God sent His son.
He came as a babe, in lowly style,
His purpose unfolding all the while.
He came to show His Father's hand -
In ways that we could understand.

He came from the Godhead - in flesh -
So that man might see His love afresh.
His message is still the same today;
To God - there is no other way -
But to trust in Jesus' sacrifice,
For forgiveness - He has paid the price!

He suffered and died, that we might live -
And rose again, His power to prove -
Power over life and death, for all
Whom He created - great and small
His handiwork around us proclaims
Miracles of nature - an anthem of praise!

Whilst here on earth, our example was He
To be servant to others in humility.
To show that self must be put aside -
Love for others shows no pride;
The first shall be last (and vice versa) He said,
He stood previous thinking *upon its head*!

So the millennium can remind us
Whatever may lay behind us
Good or bad - right or wrong -
For our Lord we must be strong.
His word as guide and His peace in our heart
The 21st century may be only the start . . . !

Dorothy Limbert

HEAR ME LORD
(For my daughter Laura truly one of God's special people)

Dear Father forgive me
For all I have said and done
I thought I did not need you
I thought that I was strong
Dear Father please forgive me
I know that I was wrong
I need to start afresh oh Lord
My heart can't stand the weight
I have to do it now oh Lord
Before it is too late
My youth was spent on nothing
The next years got much worse
And looking back I realise
I was my own bad curse
I am frightened of my Judgement Day
To stand before you on my own
To be told of all the wrong I have done
When I thought I was alone
I know you have always been with me
When I sinned and when I lied
I know that it is impossible
For me to run and hide
I can't promise you my goodness
But I will do all I can
Please remember
When you judge me
That I am only a lost man

Walter McGoff

WHAT WAS THAT?

Imagine if you will for a minute,
This moment in time and in space,
Just think of all the past history,
That happened in this very place.

Did a meteor drop from the heavens,
    did dinosaurs wander and roam?
Did a sabre tooth once have its lunch here,
    did a caveman once make it his home?
Did someone live here in the Bronze Age,
    did they know it all couldn't last?
Did they see the end coming before them,
    did they see the first Iron die cast?
Did a Viking walk through our kitchen,
    did he pillage the house that was here?
Did a Norman once put his tent up,
    did a Roman come anywhere near?
Did a boar hunt pass by my front window,
    did bloody great battles ensue?
Did Knights win hands of fair maidens,
    did Christians clash head on with Jew?
Did Cavaliers drink at the roadside,
    did Roundheads camp on my lawn?
Did the Plague claim any poor victims,
    did anyone duel here at dawn?
Did a nobleman ride past on his filly,
    did a peasant die here quite unknown?
Did a soldier return from the war zone,
    did a widow have to carry on alone?
Did forests or woodlands once live here,
    did my garage flood once every spring?
Did bluebells cover my veg patch,
    did warblers and skylarks once sing?
Did anyone rich ever live here,
    did anyone ever get killed?

Did anyone first fall in love here,
did anyone's blood become spilled?
Did treasure get buried around me,
did ill gotten gains go astray?
Did someone once dig up a fortune,
did farmers grow barley and hay?
Did livestock once graze in my greenhouse,
or did chickens once roost in my shed?
Did milking take place on my doorstep,
or did something else happen instead?
Did a balloon once descend on my rooftop,
did a birdman once prove we can't fly?
Did a man invent a new gadget,
did a child who was lost start to cry?
Did a Spitfire fly up above me,
did a Lancaster fall from the skies?
Did a woman stand here in amazement,
did a tear start to well in her eyes?
Did they ever stop to consider,
did they know how things would turn out?
Did they ever think of the future,
did they wonder what life's all about?

John R Jones

TWO THOUSAND YEARS

The mist fell over the village
blotting out the moon.
The people rushed to their windows
saying, 'Why is it dark so soon.'

A voice spoke out from the mist and said,
'Repent while you still have time,
give up your life of indifference,
debauchery and crime.'

But another voice screamed out to them,
'Don't listen to this Messiah,
if you do, I'm the Prince of darkness
and I will destroy you in the great fire.'

Then the first voice replied in a whisper,
'My people do not be afraid,
start your day with simple prayer
and the evil one will be slayed.'

The Devil hissed back his venom.
'God's words are just idle boast,
just simply ask Him the question
where were you when we needed you most?'

But during minute of silence,
a new born baby was heard,
thanking God for the gift of life,
though it couldn't yet say a word.

My friends! This could be your village,
for I haven't yet given it a name,
your town, your county, your country,
no matter they all mean the same.

Two thousand years of forgiveness
all hang on a slender thread,
don't hesitate, join in Christ's crusade,
or you will find that your soul will be dead.

Gerry Concah

GIVE THANKS

Help me Lord to ever be
Thankful for your love to me
Count my blessings day by day
Filled with your great joy, I pray
Each new morning give to you
Praise for all that you will do
As the day unfolds for me
I know that by my side you'll be
Whate'er it brings, remind me Lord
Give thanks - it tells me in your word
In all things whether good or bad
Times which are happy, sad or glad
When my heart is feeling low
This one thing I surely know
Remember your great love for me
Then forever thankful I will be

B Howard

ST GILES - OR IS IT ST ANYCHURCH?

How do we justify its low level of use?
A bit like an orange that's run out of juice
I refer to Elkesley's church of St Giles
Declining congregation, it's written in the files.
The restoration has gone on throughout the years
And there's still more to do, or so it appears
It started with a rebuild on the north aisle
Then the tower and belfry, they took a while
More fund-raising with the Christmas draw
Then the Buttermarket raised some more
Still more is needed as the roof starts to leak
The buckets and bowls must be emptied each week
It's raining in places it didn't really ought to
Could this be the source for pure Holy water?
The walls are peeling, the salt's coming through
No children come in to see what we do
They don't pick up a prayer book to read the phrases
Or open a hymn book and sing the Lord's praises
Where did we go wrong when we left them alone?
Or do they ring God on their mobile phone?
Maybe that's why they never come to church
And the vicar and wardens are left in the lurch
Or is it the parents who couldn't give two hoots
As they do the rounds on the Sunday car boots?
So please Lord help us to redress the balance
As maybe you could give us one more chance.

Stanley Swann

BALNAKEIL OUR HIGHLAND CEMETERY

On hallowed ground I stand today,
    and pause a moment while I pray.
I wait until my senses tell
    that those I visit know me well.
That those who've lain for many a year
    have mingled with the ones so dear
who left us on this tempestuous shore
    and found their peace for evermore.
From stone to stone I seem to glide,
    o'er names and places my eyes slide.
I stop beside a much loved bard,
    and concentrate so very hard,
as if to do so he would know
    how much I will my skill to grow,
to find the words with which to give
    love and comfort to those who live.
In lighter vein I take the path
    that leads to one who caused much wrath
and as I stand beside his tomb
    I think about what was his doom.
I much prefer to think of him
    with merry eye and never grim,
Not classed as outlaw here,
    but he who brings a happy cheer
when all meet here.
My visit o'er I take my leave,
    and we, the living, must not grieve,
for those within this peaceful home
    have found they have no need to roam.

Janet Parkes

JOHN 14 V 12 . . . A PARAPHRASE

Truly, truly, I say to you,
If you believe in me
You will do the works that I do,
And greater works than these you will do,
Because I go to the Father.

Ask for anything in my Name
And I will give it to you.
Yes, ask for anything in my Name;
Because the Father honours my Name
and He will give it to you.

When the Spirit of Truth shall come
He'll lead you into all truth.
The Comforter the Father will send
And He will be with you to the end,
The Holy Spirit of Truth.

No, I will not abandon you
Though I must leave you now,
But I will still be present with you;
You'll live in me and I'll live in you,
If you love and obey me.

Now a gift I give unto you,
Peace for your heart and mind.
So don't be troubled, don't be afraid,
Remember all the things I have said,
And one day you will believe me.

Sylvia Clement

THE WAY TO WALK

I heard the Voice of Heaven say,
'See, all for you I've done.
Creating Light more wondrous than
the stars, the moon, the sun;
Redemption's power to lift you up
from darkness and the mire,
To light your path, make strong your way,
all as your needs require?'

I heard the Voice of Heaven say,
'Come to My joy and peace,
To all My saving love and grace,
great riches ne'er to cease;
To heaven's fellowship divine,
My presence evermore,
My strength, power and authority
which on you I'll outpour.'

I heard the Voice of Heaven say,
'Go to My Word today
Seeing My wisdom, truth and love,
learning My will obey;
I'll show to you the way to walk
in fellowship, in grace
With Me, My own, communion's peace,
in worship and in praise.'

Ken Millar

THE FACE OF GOD

When I see the face of God
My eyes will rest at last,
Upon the one who rescued me
From my sinful past,
Who saved me from a wasteful life
And finally set me free,
He gave the world His Only Son
To save a wretch like me.

When I see the face of God
I will know that I am home,
Safe and sound and in His care
In the place that I belong,
Purchased by the sacred blood
Paid that I could be set free,
A crown of thorns, a spear of hate
To save someone like me.

When I see the face of God
As I stand before His throne,
And angels sing with one accord
To welcome me back home,
To one of many mansions
My Father has for me,
My heart is filled with love unknown
The love that set me free.

Mike Smith

FROM MANGER TO CROSS

Lord Jesus, born of Mary
Was in a manger laid,
And kings came forth to worship Him -
The tiny Heavenly Babe.

He dwelt in Nazareth village
And played on quiet hilltops,
And learned to be a carpenter
In Joseph's woodwork shop.

He toiled there with his father
With hammer, saw and plane,
One day He went a journey
And to the city came.

He sojourned in the temple
And taught the people there,
And walked among the olive groves
In quiet and fervent prayer.

He came to earth to save us,
But we cried 'Crucify!'
And hung Him on a rough-hewn cross
And left Him there to die.

Yet steadfast through the ages
Beyond His death and pain
He calls men still to follow Him
Because He rose again.

Frances Reed

ANOTHER HOLY WILLIE'S PRAYER
(With apologies to Robert Burns)

Dear God and Father,
                Hear my prayer,
I thank you for your ear,
I know you love to hear my voice,
Unlike some others here.

I am good, respectable,
A decent, upright man,
Unlike the vast majority
Who cheat whene'er they can.

I know I'm scarcely popular:
Quite frankly I don't care.
They're jealous that I'm going to heaven,
And fear they won't get there.

The poor deluded hypocrites!
I don't know why they come,
And raise their hands and sing their hymns,
As though you were their chum.

But pardon, Lord, I do digress,
It's back to me and mine.
I know your gifts are for the blessed;
Not cast before the swine.

So this is what I want, and this,
And then there's that. Now then,
Don't disappoint me, Father God.
I do deserve the best,
                Amen.

George Newall

GREAT EXPECTATIONS

Great Expectations;
That's what everyone has of me.
Expected to this,
Do that,
Live this way,
Dress like that.

Great Expectations;
What do I expect of me?
Do I expect to live
To their dreams?
I can only fail
To do that.

Great Expectations;
I must change, for me.
Do things to love
To please
Myself and God
And to be content.

Great Expectations;
That's what God has of me.
Expected to be happy
To laugh, to smile,
To love others
And to love him.

Carol A Laing

LOVE IS

Love is patient, love is kind
Makes you feel you belong
Never alone or left behind
Love is caring, love is giving
A special gift from our Father in Heaven
Love is going the extra mile
Stopping to chat with someone awhile
Love is loving when hurt appears
Keeps no records of wrongs and dries our tears
Love is accepting us the way we are
Jesus loves that way His hands stretched across the bar
So let us love each other in that special way
Throughout the years to come
Not just today.

I McDonald

UPHOLD ME LORD

Lord grant me wisdom to understand
        the needs of all I meet today
and equip me to offer a helping hand.
Grant me a listening ear to hear your voice
        and comforting words
to make the sad rejoice.

Grant me vision to seek the lost and distressed,
        guide my feet that I may
console their unhappiness.
If I should stumble along the way
        then lift me up Dear Lord I pray;
whate'er the problem, large or small,
encourage and uphold me if I should fall.

Malcolm F Andrews

THE UNIVERSE IN THE ATOM

I sat and looked at an atom and pondered its construction.
Its elemental particles orbiting about a point.
And suddenly I was looking at the Universe
From the point about which everything else rotates.

From this point of rest I was able to see everything,
But everything in the Universe.
Our Earth, which is but a minute particle in the Atomic Universe
Stood out sharp and clear.

At that point is concentrated everything,
But everything that ever was created.
All the emotions of the Universe are concentrated there.
Love, hate, jealousy, compassion, lust, forgiveness
Are there concentrated to such an extent that they materialise.

Emotions become organic objects, they take on form.
Everything but everything emanates from this point
Situated at the centre of the Universe.
If you dwell at that point you are at rest.
Peace prevails.
The atom will never look the same to me again.
The centre of the Universe is the centre of the soul
And there you will find the Kingdom of Heaven,
The Kingdom of God.

Robert E Ford

When I Was Down He Helped Me

My life was full of dark despair
There seemed no point at all
In carrying on the struggle
As on each mountain climbed I'd fall

Each day a new knock put me down
There seemed no end to pain
Then suddenly through the torment
Once more came love again

But this love came from Jesus
Who in His wisdom saw my grief
And sent His faithful servants
To offer me kind relief

And when I saw the kindness offered
And the joy with which it was given
I knew then my life had been a test
From which the sad times now were driven

My life then changed from that day forth
For now I know that people care
From the simple words as told to me
'For you! We said a prayer'

Don Woods

THANK YOU FATHER

Thank you
For being there
at my birth for
Your Breath as You
Blew life into me
For the tenderness of
Watching over me
I could not understand
Why I had to survive the
Bombing of London
The blood, the wetness
The muck and the mire
Yet You had a purpose
Then, as You have now
All my life You've watched
and waited, till at last
I turned to You through
Pouring out my brokenness to
Others and feeling the
Love in that room as I was
Held close and
Through them can at last
Understand
Why.

Pamela Smith

THE SANCTUARY

Closes the door, the traffic sounds grow dim,
The world recedes, is left far, far away;
Here but the footsteps' sound on ancient stone,
Only the murmuring of those who pray:
Take care to enter soft, tread not rough-shod;
Tread softly here, this is the house of God.

The sunlight streams upon the altar, on the cross;
The candles pale before its golden beam;
It is the light that comes out of the East,
And in its brilliance plate and chalice gleam;
And round, the watching cherubs hide their face,
That dare not look on such an act of grace.

Draw near my soul, for here is God;
Draw near, yet bow in awesome fear;
Look up, adore - O weak of faith,
Can you not know your God is near?
Around the angel hosts adore,
And you, should you not love Him more?

Close-hedged around by wings that touch
White tip to tip; and wondering eyes
That see their Lord brought low and small,
Whose blood within a chalice lies;
Whose sacred body, Heaven's light,
Beneath a veil is hid from sight.

Here then, the cross and here the throne;
The peace, the stillness and the calm;
Light from the East is pouring down,
For weary souls a healing balm;
My slumbering soul, arise, awake,
For here we kneel at Heaven's gate.

O soul, sore-chafed by daily care,
Seek thou that portion that is best;
Come to the quiet of God's house
And find His perfect peace and rest;
Here you may taste Eternity,
For God is in His sanctuary.

Daphne Foreman

AS A CHILD

As a child I stand before You Lord, stripped of all pretence,
Lost in admiration of Your vast magnificence,
You planted deep within my heart, the precious seed of love,
That blossomed forth and multiplied, and reached to You above,
You drew me close as time went by, and forged a powerful link,
Then turned the water into wine, and bade me come and drink,
I thirsted after righteousness, and hungered for Your word,
The Holy Bible opened up the glory of the Lord,
I cast my cares upon You, placed burdens at Your feet,
You lent me grace, and gave me strength for each new day to meet,
You poured Your mighty spirit out to those who would receive,
I came and took Your blessing and truly did believe
That Jesus is our saviour, so gentle, meek and mild,
I come and stand before You Lord, and worship as a child.

A Hausrath

MEDIEVAL ARGUMENT

(There was serious dispute in medieval times
as to the number of angels who could dance
on the point of a needle)

Dance, dance, dance little angels
The livelong day
Dance, dance while learned men count you;
How many, say?
While disputation rages
Grave men grow grey.
(Dance, dance, dance little angels
The night away.)

Dance, dance, dance little angels;
How can they know
On the point of a needle, how many angels
Dance to and fro?
But while they argue, can't they imagine
It might be so,
That angels grow weary; and the point of a needle
Might become painful
To an angel's toe?

Must we keep dancing?
So long a-dancing?
Tell, us not so?

Rest, little angels, rest from your dancing;
Grey men stopped counting
Long years ago.

F Jones

OUT OF DARKNESS INTO HIS WONDERFUL LIGHT

*(For you were once darkness, but now you are light in the Lord -
Ephesians 5:8)*

Jesus, hear me, take me, cleanse me
Make me Thine as Thou wouldst have me be
For child of Adam I am fallen
Yes bound by sin, a sinner me
Cut off, in darkness, ought I merit
Oh Lord I need Thy child to be
Jesus heard me, took me, cleansed me
Made me His as He would have me be
Freed from sin, the chains have fallen
Yes Hallelujah I am free
Washed by *His Blood*, clothed in *His Spirit*
Saved, free I stand, *Lord* thanks be to *Thee*
Free, nay *Jesus* hold me, never set me free
Keep me bound forever by Thy love to Thee
For I would be fearful now should I be
Loosed from the bonds of Thy love by Thee
So *Lord* keep steady the rope of Thy grace
As I grasp it to climb keep my gaze on Thy face
Up, up life's mountain so rough and so steep
In strength, mercy, love, Thou wilt carry Thy sheep

D E B

THE STORM

I was wakened by the thunder sounding far, far away,
And the lightning through my eyelids I could see;
In the middle of the night it was flashing bright as day
And lighting up the sky from A to Zee.
I counted, in the silence, from the sudden daylight flash
To the rumble of the thunder once again -
One mile, two, three, four, another clash
As cloud bumped into cloud to start the rain:
From a soft and gentle hiss to a steady rushing roar
The raindrops fell with speed down to the ground,
They spattered on the leaves and on the windows and the door
Revealed by flash of lightning all around:
Thunder cracked the air right above my startled head
As the storm advanced along its chosen way,
The rain began to slow down to a whisper as it fed
The earth before it gradually moved away
To places new, following the path of the receding thunder
As once more lightning raced from east to west,
The silence fell, and once again the sense of awe and wonder
Filled my mind with thanks for being blessed
By the majesty and glory of the symphony of rain
With percussion from the storm clouds as they lower:
The music of the heavens is a stirring, grand refrain,
The sight and sound of God's almighty power

J Moore

MILLENNIUM!

Two thousand years we have traversed
Since God's redemption plan:
Sent forth His own Beloved
To redeem all sons of man.

Many souls have been reclaimed,
Since the thief at Calvary:
His Son of righteousness eclipsed,
That His love might reach to me.

So as we celebrate millennium,
We praise Him for the light,
Still available to all men,
To disperse sin's darkest night.

How many days of grace are left,
'Til He shall come again?
And all souls by Him redeemed,
Shall forever with Him reign.

So put not off 'til tomorrow,
What you should do today,
For your procrastination,
Will determine your eternal day!

G Walford Davies

A NODDING ACQUAINTANCE

Out of the darkness of night,
Comes the first light of day,
Why? O daughter of Zion,
Why did you walk away?

Was it that life overwhelmed you,
You decided you just couldn't stay,
Or was it the next set of troubles,
That sent you on your way?

The burdens of life we shared,
Joys and happiness too,
Until O daughter of Zion,
You were bowed down with cares.

No more morning greetings,
To stop and talk awhile,
To sing and praise and dance.
Just a nodding acquaintance.

After the darkness of night,
Comes the first light of day,
When O daughter of Zion,
Will you return to stay?

Sandra Voyce

LONELY?

Dear Lonely Heart, you have a friend in Jesus,
Who one dark night was with a kiss betrayed.
With His arrest, His so-called friends all left him,
And at His trial, false witnesses arrayed.

Dear Lonely Heart, you have a friend in Jesus,
For you, endured the scourging and the pain.
A crown of thorns, and in a robe arrayed Him,
To mock and taunt, to strike Him once again.

Dear Lonely Heart, you're not alone, forsaken,
He suffered more than you will ever know.
His pierced hands, His feet and body broken,
His pierced side - His wounds forever show.

Dear Lonely Heart, He by His God forsaken,
The lonely cross, His punishment and shame.
Then all our sins, our burdens He has taken,
For through His death, our great salvation came.

Dear Lonely Heart, betrayed, beset and broken,
You've suffered much - but not as much as He,
Just trust in Him, for Heaven's but a token,
Of joy to come, when loved ones we will see.

W McIntyre

WHEN THERE WAS GRASS ON CALVARY

When there was grass on Calvary,
     as there had always been,
the elders, scribes and Pharisees
     considered it too green.

With practised guile and subtle tongues
     they warned their overlords
that the Messiah posed a threat -
     they feared His way with words.

The Roman authorities were urged
     the living grass to kill:
the rabble-rousing temple priests
     used their malicious skill . . .

Caiaphas and the Sanhedrin
     heard witnesses condemn,
but though of treason innocent
     Christ would not answer them.

Accused of public blasphemy
     and challenging the State,
on trial He refused to speak,
     and silence sealed His fate.

And on the hill of Calvary
     as Jesus there hung dead,
beneath His cross no more grew grass,
     and once-green ground was red.

Glynfab John

THE FACE OF JESUS

This story you can trace
using the Bible as your base.
Vivid illustrations there to glean,
Reflections of Jesus' face clearly seen.

Baby Jesus in his arms, Simeon's proclamation:
'Mine eyes hath seen they salvation' -
in his prayer of acclamation
as he sees *a saving face.*   Luke 2:30

Shadows hovering over Jerusalem yonder
still Jesus presses on, no time to ponder.
His sights are fixed
forging ahead; nothing betwixt,
with *a steadfast face.*   Luke 9:51

Like a sheep before her shearers is dumb,
He faced His accusers in the Judgement Hall.
He openeth not His mouth, beneath the rafters tall,
Reflecting *a silent face.*   John 19:9

Hours later, on that fateful day,
the skies turned a thunderous grey.
Calvary the crucifixion place
reveals *a scarred face.*   John 19:10 onwards

On Judgement Day before His throne,
every knee shall bow - you won't be alone.
Pictured here is *a solemn face.*   Rev 20:11

J Henderson Lightbody

CHRIST'S DEVOTION

I wish all days could be this calm,
Where peace takes o'er despair;
I wish that life held no upsets,
No frets, no tears, no cares.

But would we all appreciate
This calm if it were true?
For tears and frets and cares and all
Are what moulds me and you.

Variety is what we get
With nature and with man:
And if life held all sweetness here
No one would give a damn.

For we'd be lost in some soft world:
There'd be no need for sharing.
But when we do experience hurt,
It makes us much more caring.

So Heaven is the place to be,
For peace and angel feathers
And sunny climates all the time:
It comes through life's endeavours.

So grafting on through trials and all
Should surely bring promotion:
Not on Earth, but when we fall.
The bonus: Christ's devotion.

Kathleen Y Ambler

THE BATTLE

In the stillness of the night
The Prince of Darkness comes out to fight
The battle he thinks already won
But the battle has only just begun.

He comes to pierce our heart and mind
Of every nation and of every kind
Problems of life he likes to create
With people's lives causes heartache.

But a new day is dawning
The spirit of life in the morning
He has a future and a plan
For every woman and every man.

It cleanses us from every sin
Just ask the Lord to let him in
It frees our hearts, it frees our mind
Of every nation of mankind.

So let His spirit take control
To cleanse your soul and make it whole
No more worries, no more strife
When He has control of your life.

K Ferguson

EMMANUEL - (GOD WITH US)

Christ came to earth two *millenniums* ago
The love of God the Father to show
While here He lived a sinless life
Midst all the turmoil, trouble and strife

All hail to the *Christ*, human yet Divine
From eternal realms, yet subject to time
Born of a Virgin, miraculous birth
No other like it in all the earth

Jehovah, omnipotent, omniscient God
Veiled in flesh His creation He trod
King of Kings, Lord of Lords
Incarnate *Jesus,* yet *Eternal Word*

Deity clothed in human form
With true humility to adorn
Incomprehensible - beyond finite thought
This wondrous work that *God* has wrought

Born on earth for man's salvation
To save from eternal loss and damnation
Through *Christ* alone is forgiveness of sin
True peace of mind and cleansing within

As the end of the second millennium draws nigh
We're assured of His *coming again* in the sky
The signs of the times show it could be quite soon
Be prepared to meet Him, for unprepared could mean doom.

R B McK

THINK TWICE

Think of the solemn soul-rending request
When a faithful father was put to the test
Take thine only Isaac the son you love
Offer him in Moriah where I tell you of
For a burnt offering so clearly stated
Now, the present time plainly indicated
The call of his new name with promises due it
Reinforced his faith giving strength to do it
'Abraham' declared father of many nations
By covenant established for generations
In Isaac surely his seed would be blessed
He believed God on him did he rest
By faith he offered up his son
With God death had never won
From whence in figure he received him
God honoured faith that had believed him
Abraham, Abraham reverberated in the air
An angel intervened, his son to spare
Instead of his son the ram was burned
As Abraham said 'He and the lad returned.'
Now think of God's solemn request 'Who will go'
To be our substitute, because he loved us so
His only son answered in obedience 'Send me'
The Lamb of God's providing died on Calvary's tree
Two thousand years of grace should set hearts ablaze
Now and forever with thankfulness and praise

Sarah Smeaton

GOD ON EACH SHOULDER

What keeps us warm when the ill wind's colder?
It's the Heavenly touch of God on each shoulder.

It's just like the man who was running a race
And with the leaders he had no place.
The minutes were passing and all seemed lost
The prize could be his, but what would it cost?

A great lot of effort, a great lot of strength -
As his weary feet, covered each measured length.
And so on the track he knelt down to pray -
Though he knew the pause, was another delay.

Up to the Heavens he prayed to his God
To speed on his feet o'er the green earthy sod.
'Please O my God, let me gain renown
You lift them up, and I'll put them down.'

The long-distance runner, dry tongued with the thirst,
Could hardly believe that he came in first.
The crowd then surged forward to say 'Twas well done'
Many claps on the back, his last race he had won.

Glorious, triumphant amidst his contenders,
He had matched them all the title defenders.
And as he stood there to receive his award
He began to remember, when times were so hard.

He thought on the miles with feet that were aching,
All through his career, defeat was heartbreaking.
When he asked for help, God answered his prayer
So long ago, he should've known He was There.

From a boy to a man, now twenty years older
His great prize of all, was God on each shoulder.

Mary Josephine Devlin

VISION

Look up!
The view is better there.
Look up!
And lift your heart in prayer.
Look up!
To see a God of love;
Look up!
And trust the One above.

Look down,
And see the circumstance.
Look down,
To leave it all to chance.
Look down,
And watch the mire enclose,
Look down,
Your nakedness expose.

Look round,
To see the darkness shroud.
Look round,
And watch that great black cloud.
Look round,
Just fear the enemy,
Look round,
And find no friend to see.

Look up!
His love is always there.
Look up!
His purposes He'll share;
Look up!
The darkness disappears.
Look up!
And Jesus' blood appears.

Patricia Davies

THE MILLENNIUM AND NATURE

Can the millennium cause us pain
        With computers and their kind?
This may or may not happen
        We cannot yet define.

But nature keeps its course
        When wintertime is o'er
Then spring will be upon us
        With brighter days in store.

Then the glad beams of summer sun
        The new millennium to greet,
We all will view the lovely scene,
        Our joy will be complete.

We look forward to the autumn
        To see the colours bright,
The red, brown, green, and olive
        Though seen in fading light.

So the millennium will not spoil
        Our happy seasonal scenes,
Rather the pleasant celebrations
        Will enhance the natural themes.

To God we give our praises
        He planned the seasons well,
With crops, and fruit, and weather
        To all His will to tell.

So in the new millennium
        May we serve Christ the Lord,
And so extend His kingdom
        According to His word.

E Smith

THE MICROSCOPIC SOUL

Squeezed from the pore of human flesh,
I hovered above a mountain range of
Fleshy slopes and craggy bones.
Ecstatic at the revelation,
Released from the body's incarceration,
I was to be taken home.

I stretched my delicate transparent arms
And felt my crown of silver curls,
Caressed my lower golden fleece
And touched my face of polished pearl.
All sense of blood and nerves had gone,
Shed in that temporal case.
Caught suddenly in magnetic breeze
I was drawn at speed to outer space.

There was no sense of time or travel,
Though yellow beads of stars shot past.
Heat nor cold could penetrate
The protected shield of God's caress.
I left the galaxies behind
Without cosmic sensation.
Impatient to be reconciled
With the Master of creation.

Ahead a shining mist appeared:
Shimmering fleeces of silver and gold.
They took me to the holy spot.
I sat perfected with blissful crowds.
A paternal voice pervaded,
Welcomed me back to the shrine.
I was safe, complete, contented.
All evil I'd known was left behind.

Ken James

HE'S MINE!

(Fear thou not; for I am with thee; be not dismayed;
for I am thy God: I will strengthen thee; yea, I will help thee;
yea, I will uphold thee with the right hand of My righteousness')

He sat there in the corner,
In a big and old armchair,
Singing: 'The Lord is my Shepherd,'
Why need I fret or care?

When troubles come or sorrow,
Or illness comes to call;
The Lord is my Shepherd,
So I needn't fear at all!

As a child, I watched in wonder,
And I saw that God is real;
He is loving and He's faithful,
And He'll never, never fail!

God's presence made the difference
In his life from day to day;
I was drawn to his Saviour,
And now I too can say:

The Lord is my Shepherd,
And I shall not want, I know;
In life, in death, forever,
I have Christ where'er I go.

Even though the way's not easy,
He is with me through it all,
To uphold, and help and strengthen,
And answer when I call.

So if you don't yet know Him
As your Saviour and your Friend,
The Lord my Saviour, Shepherd,
I can truly recommend.

Joy Patterson

ETERNAL TREASURE

Money makes the world go round they say,
Always striving for more and more each day.
Working from early morn to late at night,
Tired and exhausted, not a healthy sight.

Nothing is ever enough, is our lament,
Just a little bit more and we'll be content.
Until we set ourselves another goal,
Again we fall prey and lose control.

Trying to climb the ladder to success
Often we fail and end up in a mess.
One step forward, two steps back,
Always something we seem to lack.

Seek ye first His Kingdom, Jesus said,
And we'll find sufficient for our need.
Take Him at His Word today
Peace of mind and heart we will portray.

Where your treasure is your heart will be,
God grant us wisdom to foresee,
When we build for our Kingdom in Heaven
Nothing there will ever destroy or weaken.

I Campbell

UNTITLED

Here stands this old world with all its troubles
Sorrow, pain, conflict and woe
When I gaze at a newborn baby
Often I wish that it should know
Know of the dangers, perils galore
Lying in wait on its prey to devour
Born in sin tho' so beautiful and fair
Soon this old world will present its own snares
When language develops, swear words can appear
Then on to school, temptations are there
From schooldays to college or work in a place
Night-life and social events
Can lead to disgrace
Often romance followed by marriage
Wrong choices here, mistakes we can't e'er erase
Life's doomed with misery, no happiness found
Till Jesus doth enter, sweet His name sounds
A Saviour to save us from all of our care
A harbour to rest and lower, our anchor there
Only then doth the light shine, peace doth abound
Sins all forgiven, this lost sheep's been found
Above is the sad tale of one's life so dear
Don't let it be your tale, accept Jesus now
Young boy, young girl
Salvation is free . . .
Dear Mother, dear Father
Share it with your children, as they sit upon your knee.

'Sorrowmum'

AIR GUNS

I hear a sound
And my heart just dies
Then another sound
And a painful cry
The boredom boys
Are at it again
Some poor creature
Is killed or maimed.

I go and look
At the damage done
And curse the man
Who invented the gun
Out of sheer boredom
They kill and maim
It is still with us
The mark of Cain.

Boys will be boys
They stupidly say
But what if the gun
Was pointed their way
If they lost an arm, a leg
                    or an eye
Or they looked down the barrel
It was their turn to die.

C Williams

WHAT TREASURES

As I stroll thru' fields o'gold,
there, but! Hovers a dragon-fly;
bespent, with glittering gems so bold . . .
what treasures are here to spy.

Pink and white wild roses, for a nosegay,
meadowsweet, so heady, just over there;
O to thank our God! For such a day,
for without Him, all this would be bare!

Now to enter the cool, cool woodland,
listen to the birds, so sweet;
foxgloves tall! Where I stand,
and ferns so cool, caress my feet.

In a clearing, the sun shafted pure gold,
thru' spangled silver-birch trees;
fairies gather here! I'm told . . .
to sing a song of wonders beyond compare.

Butterflies alight, like flowers, bright,
lichen, velvets every stone;
to soften footsteps in the night,
by the light of the silvered moon.

Bernard Williams

TO MY SON, FRANCIS

I'd build a bridge betwixt us my love,
Though you are there in Heaven above,
And the gap between is so very wide
For I am still on this other side.

The span it must cross is beyond my power,
So as I think of you hour by hour,
My bridge can only be in my head,
But it fills the divide and to you I am led.

There are others too, very dear to me;
I see them all in my memory,
My father and mother and brothers four;
You are all in God's keeping, I ask no more.

Your memory, my son, is more precious to me
Than anything I own, whatever it be.
I remember your smile, your ever-loving way,
The hugs and the kisses we all got every day.

It is true the afflicted bring such joy;
You gave us so much my sweet, darling boy,
So until we meet again, you and me,
I'll see you on the bridge in my memory.

Marlene Allen

MIRACLES

As Jesus walked in Galilee
A blind man found that he could see.
A lame man found that he could walk
When Jesus heard their fervent plea.

When Lazarus was laid to rest,
His sisters called on Jesu's name
And wept for joy with all the rest
When to their aid the Master came.

Then Lazurus, for all to see
Then left the grave alive and well,
As back from death he was set free,
Another miracle to tell!

The miracle I long to see
Is our world from all wars set free
And everyone received with grace
What e'er the colour of their face!

Two thousand years have now passed on
And yet we haven't learnt to give
The message from God's only son
That here in peace we're meant to live.

It matters not the way we pray
Our dear Creator needs to see
As long as we can truly say
In praise to Him, we bend the knee!

Marguerite Brassington-Griffiths

THE PARABLE OF THE RICH FOOL
(Luke 12: 13-21)

My corn is ripe, my fields are green
No better harvest have I seen.
This year I've had a good return,
All free from worry and concern.

My crops are great, my barns are few!
What shall I do?
I'll build a new, a bigger, better storage place,
My fortune says - I need the space.

And then at home I'll sit at ease:
Eating and drinking as I please.
My store will last for many years;
I'm rich, it's great I have no fears!

That night this selfish man he died,
And no one mourned, and no one cried.
The fool exchanged the gift of health
For trivial things the world calls 'wealth'.

And so I say to you, be wise,
Consider hard and realise.
Don't hoard and store for moths and rust,
Such fools as he, they all go bust!

So listen carefully unto me,
'Wherever your treasure - your heart will be'.

James Henry Jones

GOD COMES DOWN

Christ the Son came to a manger where the ass and oxen feed
God's only plan for Him to be the answer to man's need
For Satan in the garden had told Eve such a lie
He questioned God's own statement - 'Surely you will not die?'

Eve in her disobedience led Adam thus to sin
So God sent down His only son - who died man's soul to win
He came down as a baby - no doubt he gave great joy to all those who
Had gathered to view Mary's baby boy
Not knowing that within that stall lay Christ - their Lord and king
In spite of what the shepherds had heard the angels sing.

So as this Christmas we prepare our feasts of celebration
May we take time to think again of God's love for the nation
Oh how He wants each one to know His mercy, love and grace
Since for each one who trusts in Him, He has a prepared place.

'He'll come again and we can know we will view Him face to face
Thanking Him that He did come down to take the sinner's place
We will reign with Him in glory when our earthly race is run
If we've placed our trust in Jesus, God's one and only son.

S McCloskey

GOD'S PRESENCE

I went to a festival,
And met many strangers there.
We laughed and talked and sang,
And God was present there.

I went into the cathedral,
For communion and prayer,
All was pomp and ceremony
But God just wasn't there.

The dog and I went walking
Across the summer fields.
The air was soft and gentle,
And God was walking there.

I went into a tiny church
At time of evening prayer.
I knelt within those ancient walls
And God was kneeling there.

G A Ayling

DOUBTS

As predictable as leaves fall in autumn,
As certain as night turns to day,
Is this as you might see Him
As you kneel and softly pray?

As a figure you can't reach out to
Ethereal, mystic, divine
Or like a father hurrying to greet you
His outstretched arms The Sign.

Should you be contrite, benign,
Forgiving and free from sin,
Or do you feel He welcomes all
Accepting them as His Kin?

With all God's gifts around us
Why should we doubt at all?
Stand up and count your blessings
Though they be great or small.

Adeline J Haythorne

FINGERPRINTS

Little fingerprints you left me
I see them on the door
I won't try to remove them
Or your footprints off the floor

Your photograph stands on the table
Your smiling face I see
You seem to be telling me something
But the pain is too much for me

I used to hold you in my arms
You would sit on your daddy's knee
But God wanted an angel
So he took you away from me

The happiness you gave us
Was just for a little time
I'll keep your little fingerprints
To remind me you were mine

I'll ask the Lord to hold you
In His arms for me
I'll ask Him to hold you like Daddy did
And sit you on His knee

Now you're an angel in Heaven where
So many have gone before
But I'll keep your little fingerprints
The ones you left upon the door.

Florence Davies

ROUGH GROUND

A rocky cove
A pebbled beach
A pavement torn and cracked.
There's very little smooth terrain
Where foot can walk unrocked.
Perhaps a smooth, green, new mown lawn,
A cricket pitch so flat.
There's very little earth we walk
That isn't rough and marked.
Yet even if beneath the foot
The earth was velvet smooth,
We'd still walk on rough ground each day
With those we ought to love.
So many things are left unsaid,
So much we'd like to say,
Yet we must hush our nagging thoughts
And hold our tongues at bay.
We walk rough ground when standing still,
Words spoken oft in jest.
If only all the rough could stay
Beneath our feet at rest.

J Liggins

INFORMATION

We hope you have enjoyed reading this book - and that you will continue to enjoy it in the coming years.

If you like reading and writing poetry drop us a line, or give us a call, and we'll send you a free information pack.

Write to :-
Triumph House Information
Remus House
Coltsfoot Drive
Woodston
Peterborough
PE2 9JX
(01733) 898102